Rebuild

D0808838

Also by Mary Portas

HOW TO SHOP

SHOP GIRL

WORK LIKE A WOMAN

Rebuild

How to thrive in the new
Kindness Economy

Mary
Portas

BANTAM PRESS

TRANSWORLD PUBLISHERS
Penguin Random House, One Embassy Gardens,
8 Viaduct Gardens, London SW11 7BW
www.penguin.co.uk

Transworld is part of the Penguin Random House group of companies
whose addresses can be found at global.penguinrandomhouse.com

First published in Great Britain in 2021 by Bantam Press
an imprint of Transworld Publishers

A CIP catalogue record for this book
is available from the British Library.

ISBN 9781787635166

Typeset in 12.5/15.5pt Garamond by Jouve (UK), Milton Keynes
Printed and bound in Great Britain by Clays Ltd, Elcograf S.p.A.

The authorized representative in the EEA is Penguin Random House Ireland,
Morrison Chambers, 32 Nassau Street, Dublin D02 YH68.

Penguin Random House is committed to a sustainable
future for our business, our readers and our planet. This book
is made from Forest Stewardship Council® certified paper.

1

To Mylo, Verity, and Horatio. I hope this book helps make your world that little bit better

Contents

Introduction: Why Now?

Let me tell you my pandemic story. Some of it may sound familiar.

February 2020. I'm just back from a work trip with my CEO at Portas Agency, Caireen. We've been in Melbourne, Australia, where there was growing concern about a flu-like bug in China. Our Australian clients, a fashion company, were worrying about the deliveries of their next lines and what would happen if their stock didn't come in.

The first trickles of anxiety start.

Caireen and I get on the flight home – no masks, no nothing – and return to the office, where our finance director has a bit of a cough. We don't take much notice. It's good to be back and sharing the buzz of the trip. But the tension grows as the days turn into weeks. This flu thing just isn't going away. We can feel there's some kind of crisis coming but can't see exactly what shape it will take.

Soon, one of our team – whose husband is in politics – comes in and tells us that Boris Johnson, the prime minister, is going to lock down the UK. And we still can't really envisage what the crisis will look like, even though we are on the point of walking into it.

We have a last afternoon in the office, and the whole team gets together to open up the beer and wine. The mood is slightly absurd, almost end-of-term. 'We'll be back in a month, so let's have a good drink.'

We are laughing and a bit giddy. It's surreal. The atmosphere is a mix of fear and slight excitement at something so unlike anything we've known before. It's a bit of a novelty. And the weather is going to be great in April, apparently. So we all go home and go into lockdown and try to figure out how to look professional on Zoom calls.

A few days later Caireen rings me and says: 'OK, so our clients in the States and in Australia have stopped work.'

'What do you mean, stopped?'

'Just closed down for now.' These are retail clients and they have shut their doors.

I can't process it properly. 'So what does that mean? What does it mean for us?'

'It's going to be at least a few months: they have cancelled the work we were doing for them. We need to find new ways to support them.'

We start to do the maths together, and figure out we are probably going to take a 15–20 per cent hit to our immediate profits. OK, we can do this. I talk to Mark, my finance director, and we look at the staff we have, our rent and contracts, and we reckon we'll be all right. We'll be down a chunk, but all right.

Breathe. We just have to keep focus here.

Two days later another client calls, same deal. And within three weeks we go from 20 per cent down in profits through 50 per cent to 'lucky if we can manage to break even'.

Meanwhile, I'm at home with a house full of my children, old and young. In one room, my son Mylo is working from his laptop. In another my daughter Verity is doing her master's degree online. And in between I'm trying to get my eight-year-old, Horatio, to do insanely complicated maths equations as part of his virtual schooling, while fielding calls about my crumbling business.

Like any mother, I keep smiling on the surface while paddling furiously underneath. But the fear is building constantly inside me. The business that we've built up over twenty-one years, that's always been profitable, that my team and I have seen through all the storms including the 2008 crash, is on the line. The question mark now is not about the profits but sheer survival.

I am completely consumed by fear. Everything I'd relied on, had planned for the future, seems uncertain. I'm four weeks away from my sixtieth birthday – looking forward to the years when I was supposed to sit back a bit and enjoy slowing down. Just a little.

Now I'm wondering if everything is going to implode. I sleep less and less. Turning restlessly in my bed as I worry about everything we have built, and my employees' livelihoods, being at risk.

For the first time in my career, I feel completely and utterly at a loss. And it's largely because the guiding light of my whole career, which is something I can't explain, has always been a sense of what's going to be the next thing, where people are going. I've somehow always managed to work that out.

I've been a fixer, too, since my mother died when I was sixteen, my father not long afterwards, and my siblings and I were cut adrift. I've always been the one to sort things out, ride in on a white horse and save everyone. But suddenly I am completely and utterly floored. This feels too big, too unknowable. Unfixable. Like so many others, I'm wondering where my life is going to land when all this ends.

The next month brings constant bad news. And the irony is that my business involves advising others on what to do next. While other agencies are putting out think pieces about what businesses should be doing, we stay uncharacteristically silent.

We don't have a ten-point plan or snappy flow chart to

show people how to get out of a pandemic. We just don't know what to say. Nor do we really want to – yet. And I've *always* had something to say. So there I am, the weeks passing, the fear beating out of my chest, me like a pilot holding white-knuckled on to the airplane controls as I try to stop it crashing.

But slowly, so slowly in fact that I hardly realize it's there, another feeling starts to unfurl inside me: a strangely peaceful kind of acceptance. I get tired of all the fear and worry. I realize that it's not helping anything. No one knows how this will end. I'm not failing because I can't work out what to do. We're all just surviving and I've got to sit with it. All of us have got to lean into the pain and simply try to look after our people and business as best we can.

Every day, Caireen and I talk as we learn together how to be in this new reality. And as we do, there is one thing that keeps coming to the forefront of our minds, an idea we've been exploring over the last couple of years – almost as a side hustle. We call it the Kindness Economy and it follows on from thinking I laid out in a book called *Work Like a Woman*.

It's about shifting the sole purpose of business from money, money, money at all costs to better protecting the earth's resources and our own wellbeing. Once we began to research this idea, we found more and more voices saying the same thing: we cannot keep going down the same path. We need to prioritize different things – the world we live in and the people who inhabit it – not just the bottom line.

The Kindness Economy is a movement for how consumer culture needs (and wants) to change. The landscape of how people buy, sell, make and live has to change. We need social progress to go hand in hand with commerce.

I gave a TED talk on the Kindness Economy back in December 2019, a couple of months before the name Wuhan became famous worldwide. As a company we'd already implemented changes and embraced more purposeful behaviours, but we weren't shouting about it. We weren't sure if we'd commit professional suicide by talking about giving back in a world that's often only about taking. Or have our values misconstrued as the marketing equivalent of virtue signalling. Some clients got it, some simply didn't – no matter how much we highlighted the jeopardy inherent in 'business as usual'.

But we're in different times now. And the pandemic gives everything we've been thinking about a new urgency. What is going to get us through is human empathy, not just clever strategies. With everything in free-fall, it's time to take some risks.

All around us we can see that, even with its awful challenges, the coronavirus pandemic has brought a recognition of the important things in life – and business: community, value, creativity and purpose. These will be our life rafts. It's never been so important. And the more I read and hear about these ideas, the more I realize that, while Covid-19 has accelerated this sense of change, the seeds were sown before we'd ever heard of it.

Greta Thunberg and the climate change activists. The brave women of #MeToo. The Black Lives Matter movement. All of them had one core message: 'We've had enough of the status quo. Things need to change.' We cannot go on exploiting the world's resources and each other and expect there to be no consequences.

Small parts of the world of business have been undergoing a quiet revolution. But now this needs to be bigger and wider. And by forcing everything so close to the edge, business will now have to find new ways to rebuild. We need to work together to benefit the greater good. It's about survival for us all.

Caireen and I talk (we talk a lot) – and come to realize that this Kindness Economy thinking is going to be the only way forward. We don't know if our clients will understand it – or even if there are going to be any clients in the future. But we just have to follow this path. This is where the truth lies. It is the only way to rebuild.

Now, I'm sure there were points in this journey where Caireen and the team wondered if I'd finally lost all sense of reason. But they believed in it. More than that – they knew it was the way forward. We'd cling on to that core instinct and see where it would take us.

We start as simply and directly as we can: a newsletter that appears in our contacts' in-boxes containing our unvarnished thoughts about how we see the future of living and buying, and how business will sit within that.

The newsletter starts with a few hundred readers – colleagues and clients – and then more people start to sign up. Soon we have 7,000 addresses on our database. It keeps growing. Businesses are reading what we're saying and getting in touch to ask for our advice. They like the new approach. They also know it makes commercial sense.

We, meanwhile, are building the ship while we're sailing it. This is all new, experimental, but that is OK. We don't have all the answers. But we are guided by the truth we all believe in. And we begin to find our way. We learn to navigate the new reality without hitting the rocks.

You'll have your own pandemic story no doubt. You will have felt the pain – both personal and professional – that we have all been through. And the other common emotion of the past year has been fear: exhausting, debilitating fear as we've tried to keep it all hanging together.

Because of that, I know that the energy needed to think

about new values and approaches may feel in short supply right now. But here's the crucial thing: the businesses out there who think this is just a nice-to-have that they can think about in a couple of years are the ones who will be left behind. Those who are going to survive and thrive will be the ones who start to adapt and reinvent right now. This is a commercial imperative. Your life raft.

Change is all around us. It won't just stop as we start to move slowly to post-pandemic life. The scars Covid leaves will take a long time to heal. But it also offers us a huge opportunity for transformation, growth and the righting of a system that has only skewed further and further off course in recent decades.

And it isn't just Covid. In any lifetime, in any business, challenges and changes will come. There will always be crises to weather. They may not be as global and radical as this one, sure, but you will still need the same tools to navigate them. The principles of the Kindness Economy are there to steer you through whatever comes, because they are there to create a better, more humane society for us all, one in which we can all be at our strongest.

We have all been fundamentally changed emotionally by the pandemic. Things will not just slip back into place and return to what they once were. We are developing new expectations and needs, new desires and priorities. And if we want to thrive in this world then we all need to embrace the kind of change that the Kindness Economy offers, interpret it within our own lives and our own businesses, and be part of a force that will transform how we all live and buy.

1

We've Been Doing It Wrong

I need to start with a hefty dose of *mea culpa*. If I'm talking about the excesses of the system, the waste and bad practices, then I have to admit I was at the epicentre of all that for a long time. To be exact, I was one of the people selling you stuff you didn't need. And I was really good at it.

In the early nineties I became the creative director of Harvey Nichols. At the time, it was the *grande dame* of department stores, frequented by older Knightsbridge ladies who dressed in classic fashion labels like Jean Muir and Bruce Old-field.

But the store was slowly dying and we needed to create a new profile that would make Harvey Nichols appeal to a wider range of people. (Well, when I say people, let's be honest, I mainly mean women, because we're the ones who mostly drive buying decisions. We also drive the majority of purchasing decisions; an important point because the power to create change often lies in our hands.)

Back to the nineties. Fashion and accessories were key to attracting women into the store and, as the creative director, I had to envision the whole environment, the atmosphere, from its displays to the marketing, advertising, events and the publicity that would create the buzz to entice people in.

So I installed art and sculpture in the windows, launched young designer catwalk shows in-store and made Harvey

Nichols synonymous with luxury fashion courtesy of a partnership with *Ab Fab*. The customers loved it, the brands loved it, the press loved it and I was truly living my best creative life. Harvey Nichols was a big, beautiful fantasyland where I could turn all my ideas into reality. But at the root of all that buzzy creative stuff, of course, was one thing: selling.

While my bosses bathed in the glory of the new cultural relevance I created at Harvey Nichols, what really overjoyed them was how much money we were making. Harvey Nichols became *the* destination department store, and one of the key aspects of this reinvention was tapping into a trend that has continued to this day: the It bag.

Before then, women had carried good-quality leather bags, if they were lucky, from M&S. But suddenly they were given access to bags, perfume and sunglasses that were an accessible entry point into the luxury brands. Accessories were burgeoning into a massive cash cow for both designers and stores.

Seeing the early signs, I knew that picking the right styles for the next season would be crucial to our bottom line. Have the right bag in-store, display and market it correctly, and people would not only come in to buy it, but also spend in other areas.

By 1995 there was no man who better summed up the new luxury than Tom Ford. As beautiful as any of the models who walked his shows, Tom Ford exuded glamour and sex appeal – and he'd infused this into the brand he was working for at the time: Gucci. Their Horsebit bags had been around for a while, but the Tom Ford sparkle dust had made them one of the season's most desired items. One beautiful example was given an entire full window to itself, spotlit to ensure the ladies who lunched couldn't miss it.

The bags get snapped up, the numbers go in the right direction and a few months later I am walking through the office when I hear one of the junior accounts assistants talking. Let's call her Emma.

'I'm so happy it's mine,' she says to the woman sitting opposite her.

Emma gazes lovingly at something beside her desk. I wonder if she's looking at her firstborn in a carrycot or something. But no. Sitting beside Emma is a Gucci Horsebit bag.

That's the moment I should have stopped, shuddered and seen the light. Emma in accounts was in her early twenties. She can't have been on a huge salary and shouldn't have felt the need to spend hundreds on a handbag she couldn't afford. There were thousands of well-made leather bags that cost a fraction of the price.

But Emma didn't want those. She wanted a piece of the Tom Ford myth, the Gucci brand, and everything that I'd done to make it desirable had encouraged her to think her life would be fulfilled by it. Instead of questioning any of this, though, I almost rubbed my hands with glee. My work was done.

So there you have it: my life as master of selling you stuff you don't need, purveyor of myths and falsehoods around material objects, convincing you that owning them will change who you are and how you feel.

The pursuit of happiness

Let me be clear: there's nothing wrong with luxury per se. You certainly have to pay more for better materials, quality and production techniques. *But* – and this is the really big but – the It bag isn't a question of one piece that will last you years. It changes every season, and the subliminal messaging behind all the marketing says God forbid you fall behind. And this restless pursuit of the new cascades out and fuels the beast that is fast fashion. Whatever you are wearing – high end, high street, mass market – becomes gauche, or so you are led to think, six times a year.

I might have moved on, but the hamster wheel of consumerism hasn't stopped; in fact, it is turning faster and faster. Where fashion once worked to two key seasons, there are now pre-seasons, cruise collections and many in between. Even the words we use to describe the products sound relentless: the must-have, must-buy, must-get bag/dress/coat of the moment. For the consumer, it's about the pursuit, the thrill of the chase, then finally the catch. And, crucially, the prices have risen and risen as appetite has grown. In 2010, a Mulberry Alexa bag would cost you £695. Now it's £1,095. The process isn't about buying something beautiful and intrinsically valuable and built to last. It's about having the right bag at the right time. If you accelerate the seasons, you accelerate consumption.

From a business point of view, it's going fabulously. The system – and all its parts, from brands to shops to media – is still teaching Emma from accounts that it isn't worth saving up to make herself financially secure and independent. Instead, she's swallowed the idea that bunging a bag she can't afford on to a credit card is 'normal'.

It isn't just fashion, either: it's everything from the need-to-have new iPhone (that's basically indistinguishable from the last one except this one needs a different plug and your headphones won't work any more, so you'd better replace all the cables) to the latest Nikes. From the new kitchen to the cool furniture. The boys' toys. The new car. Buy more, sell more. This is where your identity lies.

I didn't see it back then, but I see it now. All of this is misguided. It is misguided because underpinning it all is one main principle: that selling more stuff to create more profit and economic growth is the only thing that matters. It's a machine that has got bigger and bigger as consumerism has exploded in recent decades, and it's affected us in profound ways. Where once, up until the eighties, we mostly bought what we needed – and the odd thing that brought us joy – we're now being sold to via the idea that the coat or the bag or the car will make us feel part of the in-crowd. More than that, it'll actually make us happy. Even the people who think they're beyond being influenced by trends and glossy advertising are being oversold to. My mother darned, resoled shoes and repaired holes (anyone remember those massive leather elbow patches on their school jumpers?) in order to make things last. Today we all simply throw out and move on with a replacement. Each year £140 million worth of clothing goes into landfill.

All this consumerism has been driving the economic machine and it's wrong.

Time's up

This central tenet of rampant consumerism has been killing our planet. It has been exploiting vast numbers of people. It has been draining the only resources we will ever have. And, in its relentless drive to make us sate our anxiety by consuming more and more, it has been killing our collective wellbeing.

What I was doing back in the nineties was commoditizing Emma herself. Once we see Emma as a person, not as a commodity, we start to realize that we're all people, in this together. It is about empathy: had I treated Emma and those like her with more respect, she would have been more empowered to make her own decisions. We would have seen that the economy should be working for her, not just the businesses that use every trick in the book to sell to her. In the end, it is people who matter. The planet will keep going, one way or another. But we won't be here unless we fully understand what we are doing that is harmful and put all our efforts into harnessing our power to effect change.

The good news is that finally, over the past years, businesses have been waking up. Listen to the change encapsulated in the words of the creative director of Gucci today, Alessandro Michele: 'Our reckless actions have burned the house we live in . . . we incited Prometheus and buried Pan . . . So much outrageous greed made us lose the harmony and the care, the connection and the belonging.'

At every scale, in every sector, from banking to car manufacturing, energy providers to retailers, there is an invigorating uprush of energy and a rising chorus of voices looking at how to do things differently. New businesses embodying hugely innovative approaches are springing up. Established businesses are making giant changes. The need to take responsibility has become a prerequisite of business – for proof, just follow the money: investors are increasingly requiring that businesses take their social and environmental responsibilities seriously. (Last year, the CEO of the world's largest asset investor, BlackRock, said this in his letter to CEOs: 'Awareness is rapidly changing and I believe we are on the edge of a fundamental reshaping of finance.') And if businesses want to attract the best and the brightest to work for them, they know that they have to be serious about making change.

I love business. Fundamentally, I live and breathe it. What I love best about my work is making businesses work. And that is why, right now, I feel a huge excitement. I truly believe that business holds the power to make real and fundamental societal change. This wave that is coming is both top-down and bottom-up. Politicians have some power, but they are locked into five-year election cycles and short-term thinking. Businesses, on the other hand, are both intimately bound up with communities for the long haul and intimately bound into the energy surging up from the grass roots. We are here to serve people, and in turn we know that what people buy, how they buy, and who they buy from is a hugely powerful force. If businesses harness that force to make change, they can transform societies.

The pursuit of profit

There is now a mass questioning or reckoning underway that is allowing us – as business owners, as customers, as people – to look afresh at what capitalism could and should be. There is momentum gathering: a willingness to challenge the accepted norms of how our societies and economies are organized. If we are going to rebuild a better business landscape, if we as individuals are going to change our behaviour, we need to have faith that the world is transitioning away from traditional capitalism towards a new model that embraces cultures and values that flow from the top down. To understand this shift, we need to understand how governments of nations worldwide interpret value – and how they implement policies to reflect that.

One person who has really helped me to open my eyes further to the drawbacks of our current economic model is the economist Kate Raworth. As she points out, one huge part of the consumer culture problem is the way we measure national progress – GDP.

When the American government needed a simple metric to help them quantify what was happening during the Great Depression in the 1930s, they turned to an economist called Simon Kuznets, who gathered together all the financial transactions in the nation – all the investments made, goods bought, deals done. It's a monetary measurement. But there is a lot it leaves out.

'GDP doesn't tell you anything about the value that's created in households, it doesn't tell you about the value that's created in communities, the value that's created in society. It only tells you the value of what has been sold; it doesn't tell you the value of what's been lost. So it will only tell you the value of timber. It doesn't tell you the value of the forest that you cut down,' says Kate Raworth.

To get that straight: we put a price on units of timber, but raising children, teaching them the basics, and making sure that they grow up as responsible citizens doesn't figure? At the other end of the scale, we'll measure the ships we build but not the work done caring for our ageing parents? If it's that unimportant then I really want to see all those economists and politicians when the paycheques dry up and they're no longer 'useful'.

What GDP does do is give a simple measure that seems to tell how a country is 'doing'. Is it solvent, or in debt? Are people employed? What are they selling and buying? In doing so, it prioritizes growth above all else as a measure of a nation's success. We'll return to this later in Chapter 11, but for now it's enough to say that a lot of wise people – including Kuznets himself – have subsequently recognized that there are huge limitations to using GDP as a measure. And yet, it has endured.

The result of this is that the nations of the world have become locked into an obsessive race to prioritize economic profit and growth, without looking more deeply into whether this measure is the right one to be pursuing.

Kate's work is dedicated to getting us to rethink our desire for unchecked growth. Her brilliant theory is called Doughnut Economics – a plea for us all to view progress not in terms of endless vertical growth, but in terms of balance. She pictures the use of all the earth's resources radiating out from a central point as economies grow, forming a circular, target-shaped diagram. It's important that nobody occupies the inner circle – this is where there hasn't been enough growth; where societies don't have enough to meet their basic needs. But it is important too that once that need has been met, we don't push growth past an outer rim, past the point that our planet can tolerate.

Her ideal is that economies reach a 'Goldilocks Zone' – one where everybody globally has enough resources, and where nobody takes too much. This Goldilocks Zone is a ring, a doughnut; the sweet spot.

Right now, things are going wrong in that doughnut ring. Globally, far too many people are falling into the central hole and simply do not have enough to meet their needs. And, at the outer rim, too many of the world's finite resources are being drained.

Mark Carney, former Governor of the Bank of England, puts it like this: 'We've been trading off the planet against profit, living for today and leaving it to others to pay tomorrow.'

The man who was the head of our key economic institution is concerned that we are thinking too much about profit. (Bit of a shame that he didn't say that while he was still in the job, but better late than never.)

This trade-off has been becoming more and more clear over the last decade. The Covid-19 pandemic has thrown it into ever sharper relief, widening the inequality gap in almost all developed nations, and straining our economies to breaking point.

We have reached the point where we all fundamentally know that unchecked consumerism is damaging us. I could quote you pages of statistics to demonstrate it, but here are just a few:

- 22 per cent of the world's population live in poverty – 9.2 per cent in extreme poverty – while the top 1 per cent own almost half (43 per cent) of global wealth.

- Roughly 3.2 billion people worldwide are impacted by land degradation.

- At roughly 416 parts per million, carbon dioxide levels in our atmosphere are the highest they have been in human history.

- Even before the coronavirus pandemic struck, over 5 million people in the UK were paid less than a fair living wage – something that should be a basic entitlement.

- Half of the world's forests have been cleared, a deforestation that in itself contributes 12–17 per cent of annual global greenhouse gas emissions.

- 1 million marine animals are killed by plastic every year, while less than 9 per cent of all the plastic produced is recycled.

- 20 per cent of the world's population are responsible for the consumption of 80 per cent of its resources.

Is all of this making us happy? It seems not. Our mental health isn't better. We've got greater inequality, and it seems to be worsening, storing up problems for the next generation. In the US, the number of teens reporting the symptoms of depression increased by 52 per cent, and the figure for young adults by 63 per cent over the decade to 2017. Again, this is before the mental health crisis engendered by the pandemic.

These are the effects of a market – of a society – which venerates the concept of economic growth above all else. We still see the effects of unrestrained growth in action all around us: the drive towards accumulation for its own sake, the anxiety that results from that; the depletion of our resources, the exploitation that results; the landfill piling up in the earth. But things are changing: businesses now know that this model doesn't look so good any more. It doesn't feel so good – not to them, and not to the people buying. And this way of doing business, of consuming, of living, can't go on.

'Gradually, and then suddenly'

We know all this needs to change. A lot of clever people have been telling us this for some time. We ourselves know it. A lot of brilliant businesses are addressing it. We know it can't sit in theory. It can't just be talking heads at summits and Mark Carney giving a Reith lecture. How long is it going to take for everyone (and not just the *FT*-reading few) to get on the bandwagon? We have reached the tipping point.

We are at the moment when the snowball is picking up enough mass to become an avalanche. It's a bit like that line from a Hemingway novel, *The Sun Also Rises*; asked how he lost all his money, a character – a drunk, bankrupt war veteran – answers, 'Gradually, and then suddenly.'

We are at the cusp of suddenly. Societal shifts can happen astoundingly quickly, once they pick up critical mass.

I know all this sounds scary and daunting. But bear with me. I'll tell you a story about how quickly things can change.

Do you remember when smoking was sexy? Back in the day, my father would sit me in front of a Bette Davis movie. There she was in *All About Eve* – cocktail and cigarette in hand, jewels flashing, pure Hollywood glamour. And then, in the seventies, we had the Marlboro Man – beyond aspirational.

For me, smoking started when I left college and joined Harrods as a window dresser. I started out on Sobranies. Remember them? All the different colours, the gold filter and ridiculously expensive. We'd go across the road to Arco cafe for a cheeky one that we'd nicked from the window displays. (Imagine that – cigarettes wedged between the fingers of the mannequins in a shop window.) We'd squabble over the ones we thought looked best with what we were wearing. It was great. It was fun. We thought we were cool.

How do we picture smokers today? Huddled outside under an awning somewhere or in the road outside the pub amid the butt ends, freezing, having a fag. There is not one jot of aspiration or sex appeal involved. And all of this in a few short years.

Where did all that glamour and mystique go? Well, it went gradually, and then suddenly. We knew for years – because the scientists had told us – that smoking wasn't good for us. They had been telling us since the fifties. But somehow that just made it feel a bit illicit, a little bit more naughty. And then there were the advertising bans, and the health warnings on packets – but we didn't really pay much attention to those . . . And then there were articles and films and documentaries, and there were the smoking bans on public transport, and in offices, and so on and so on until the total ban on smoking in indoor public places in 2007. Within a couple of years of that, the thought of smoking inside – the very idea that people not so long ago used to smoke at their desk, or on a bus, or even worse on a plane – seemed totally mad.

It wasn't just the health messages, or the legislation, or the lawsuits. It was a cultural shift, one that seeped into the national consciousness, into our general bank of knowledge. There was education, and then legislation, and then the conversation. And the result is that the cigarette is no longer cool or chic or fun. The cigarette has no status any more.

And the same thing is happening with the 'more! more! more!' economy. The unthinking accumulation of stuff is losing its status – it's been happening gradually, and then all at once. The experts started talking about climate change a long time ago; they started to tell us about what we were doing to our planet and ourselves. They told us, but it didn't really sink in. Somehow we resisted the knowledge.

Then there were changes in the law and in policy. And then the documentaries and films and marches and manifestoes. There have been heroines and heroes of the movement, and there have been people working away in the background, trying to get the message across.

The Nobel Prize-winning economist Robert Shiller has a theory called Narrative Economics. He argues that the most powerful forces in our economy are the stories that seep into our culture: the conversations we have with our friends, our neighbours, our taxi drivers. The nuggets of information we all begin to share as indisputable truths. These are the forces that drive the markets, that make things happen.

And these are the stories that we are now telling ourselves. They manifest in articles, in podcasts, in Netflix series, on our social media feeds, in everyday conversation – countless stories with the same radical messages: we cannot continue endlessly piling up more and more material possessions in the service of increasing growth. There must be a better way. We need to slow down. The earth and its people cannot survive an unlimited accumulation of stuff. This relentless cycle of acquisition is not making us any happier.

This is a far bigger and more fundamental shift than the fate of the cigarette. Again, it is a mixture of education, legislation and conversation. What that conversation is saying is that we have been incentivized badly – we have been told that our lives are better if we have more stuff to show for ourselves: more tech, more clothes, more things in our houses. Cartloads of money and masses of ingenuity have been spent by the advertising industries to tell us that this is what will make us happier people. As business people we have been told we should prioritize profit to shareholders above all else, feed the psychological craving for more stuff; this in turn leads to growth; and growth is the yardstick by which we should measure our success – as people, as businesses, as societies.

It's all misguided.

As Kate Raworth says: 'When we use the earth's resources in such a way that we begin to push ourselves beyond the living capacities of this planet, we are literally undermining the life supporting systems on which we depend.'

Jacinda Ardern, the prime minister of New Zealand, puts it even more succinctly: 'Economic growth accompanied by worsening social outcomes is not success. It is failure.'

This has been the way we have been operating, as businesses, as individuals, as entire economies. But now we have some very smart people talking to us about how to reimagine. The late California senator John Vasconcellos put it beautifully when he told us that the task is to be hospice workers for the dying culture and midwives for the new: a wonderful evocation of the evolution we are experiencing. There is an upswell of people wanting things to be done differently. We have a raft of businesses wanting to try new things. It's a beautiful collision of top-down and bottom-up. Reimagining, rebuilding: this isn't out-there, pioneering stuff any more. It is, as it should be, part of the new norm. I want to show you how to be part of that vibrant, fantastic wave of recreation, because that is where all our futures lie.

TO DO

Open your eyes

In 2013, when the late writer David Foster Wallace gave a commencement speech at Kenyon College in the US, he started with a simple parable: 'There are these two young fish swimming along and they happen to meet an older fish swimming the other way, who nods at them and says, "Morning, boys. How's the water?" And the two young fish swim on for a bit, and then eventually one of them looks over at the other and goes, "What the hell is water?" '

In the last couple of years, a lot of people have started being able to see the water for the first time. And we don't always like what we see: the outlines of a lot of invisible systemic stuff – from the patriarchy, to structural racism – are suddenly coming into focus.

Just as we have opened our eyes to the flaws in our political and cultural systems, so this is the time to open our eyes to the realities of our economic systems and the damage they are doing. In *Ways of Seeing*, the great John Berger said: 'The way we see things is affected by what we know or what we believe.' What we know, what we believe, are at a point of change.

We've all been swimming through this water for a long time, without ever asking, 'Why are we swimming? Is this the right way?' Wouldn't it be wonderful to find again that feeling a child has when seeing something for the first time? We stand to gain so much by experiencing the world as if it's new.

Let's strive for that as our first step. Let's allow ourselves to feel the water. Let's judge for ourselves whether it's right for us. And if we find it too hot or too cold, not fresh enough or not clear, let's give ourselves the opportunity to change it.

2

The Covid Conscience

I believe we are living through an age of enlightenment. I believe we are in an era of hope.

I know that hope and enlightenment may feel in short supply at the moment. Certainly, even a cursory glance at the headlines over the last couple of years has been enough to send spirits plummeting – and then the pandemic. For some, the Covid year has brought irreversible tragedy and heart-break; for others, job losses and economic hardship are going to mark the years ahead. All of us have been changed and scarred. We have had to weather a storm we never could have seen coming.

But amid all this darkness, there is a momentum towards something better. I can feel it. As a society, no matter how locked down, we are in motion towards a massive shift. It has been coming for a while; just look at the movements that have bubbled up over the last few years. But Covid has been a catalyst: it has taken these elements and supercharged them.

Even with all that Covid took from us – from lives to livelihoods – I truly believe that it also gave back. The pandemic brought with it a greater sense of community. A greater need to think in terms of the whole, not of the individual. A greater understanding that the way we behave in everyday life has a real impact on the planet and everyone around us.

At the end of the last chapter, I invited you to try to open your eyes to the water we are all swimming through. But my guess is you may have already started on this journey of self-reflection. As a society, it's no coincidence that we are going through a period of re-evaluation, that movements for change are emerging in every area of our lives. Through this shared moment of forced pause, we have finally been able to stop moving long enough to look around us, and we are saying that we don't like everything we see. But we are also saying that we have the will and the power to change it. Out of chaos comes opportunity.

The author Fatima Bhutto expressed this mixture of loss, regret and dawning hope eloquently: 'Covid-19 will destroy many things, but hopefully too the broken scaffolding of our moral imagination.'

I call it the 'Covid conscience': the radical re-evaluation of what we know and what we care about in the wake of the pandemic. The age of individualism was already moving towards the exit. Covid is now ushering it out the door.

That is the enlightenment. The hope lies in the fact that Covid has taught us a hard-learned lesson: we are far more brilliantly adaptable than we knew.

Adapt and thrive

I'm standing in the freezing cold, the wind is whistling around my ears like an arctic blast and . . . I'm queuing for an ice cream.

So are loads of other people. Even deep in the Covid winter. Familiar faces from my local neighbourhood fill the queue, unable to resist the chance to wave at each other from two metres apart and prise our kids off their gadgets to get a breath of fresh air.

I can't wait for the moment when my freezing lips sink into a pistachio ice cream.

But it's not the sense of community and connection flowing between us as we stand in the cold that I'm going to focus on right now – more of that later. Instead, I want to talk about how this tiny ice-cream shop in north London sprang into life.

It's owned by two great local people, Sirine and Matt. Sirine is an actress, a very talented one, and you'll probably have seen her on telly. Her husband Matt works in events and they've got two kids. Years ago, when prices were low and normal people could get a mortgage on a place in London, they bought a flat with a shop below that they could rent out for extra income.

Now, the shop isn't in the greatest location because it's down a side street so you have to seek it out a bit. But for years there was a popular yoga studio opposite so this little street got great footfall. Then the local council voted to convert the yoga studio into those bland luxury flats with marble countertops and white walls. So the yoga studio shut down, people stopped coming and the clothes outlet that rented Sirine and Matt's shop moved on. Then Covid hit, both acting and events were shut down, and Sirine and Matt suddenly had no income coming from anywhere.

And so they did what positive, resourceful and, yes, slightly mad people do when they're up against it: they opened an ice-cream shop. Down an alleyway. In winter.

Sirine is far from juicing out every penny of her profit. She's so busy chatting and putting every imaginable sweet, sauce and sprinkling on the ice creams that she's not exactly pumping customers through the till. Meanwhile, Matt is handing out cups of tea and hot chocolate to grateful customers almost at the point of hypothermia.

But they've thrown themselves in, they're learning, and for me Reenie's Ice Cream Bar is a brilliant example of the shafts of light that shone even amid the darkness of Covid. Sirine and Matt took the best of a bad situation and turned it around. One ice cream at a time. They slapped some Dulux on the walls, bought in great-quality ice cream and set to work. In business speak, they pivoted. In normal speak, they did what they could to survive.

As did so many others, businesses small and large. Covid has taught us that businesses can quickly adapt. Regulations on social distancing measures were implemented at lightning speed. Perspex screens sprang up in every shop, bank, cafe and waiting room. Awnings and tables appeared outside pubs, at huge cost, only to be put away again as lockdown bit harder. Distilleries revved up to make hand sanitizer instead of whisky. Your local Italian restaurant redeployed itself as an outside-table delicatessen. Makeshift counters were set up in shop doorways. In the name of keeping things going, businesses have bent themselves into whatever shape they could to survive.

It's the embodiment of 'elastic thinking', a term coined by theoretical physicist and *Star Trek* writer Leonard Mlodinow. This is about harnessing the fluid power of insight and instinct, over rational, logical, analytic thought.

In retail, it was interesting to watch the positive ways in which some businesses were able to react. The grocery sector stepped up quickly, for instance. Supermarkets worked closely with government, and took on an almost institutional role. Yes, they were sitting relatively pretty being allowed to remain open, but it's fair to say that they were about more than just making a quick buck.

All of them moved at speed to prioritize the needs of NHS workers and the vulnerable, making sure they were meeting the requirements of the widest possible range of people. Asda invested £2 million into an initiative to provide 7,000 Dell laptops to schoolchildren across the UK who were unable to access remote learning. The Co-op instituted an 'I've got time to chat' badge for its delivery drivers in central England, in a bid to combat lockdown loneliness.

At the other end of the size scale, my tiny local bookshop speedily ramped up their digital presence with a click and collect service. Up against the giants of the internet, they created a new niche for themselves – a service that was responsive, reactive, and touching. Each order was beautifully wrapped with flowers tucked into the paper. When you dropped by to pick yours up, you also got a personal recommendation for another book you might enjoy. The result? Their takings went up substantially in lockdown.

I've always appreciated the role retailers can play in the lives of their customers. This past year has shown us all how powerful that presence can be. They grounded us when the ground fell away. They stayed open when everything locked down. They partnered, diversified, found ingenious ways to sell and deliver exactly what we needed in the moment we needed it most. It reminds me of some beautiful lines from the writer James Baldwin: 'For nothing is fixed . . . The sea rises, the light fails, lovers cling to each other, and children cling to us. The moment we cease to hold each other, the moment we break faith with one another, the sea engulfs us and the light goes out.'

We don't just see this at the small-scale local level, either:

retailers like John Lewis have taken this moment to broaden their role even further – exploring financial services and housing. A necessity, no doubt, after their catastrophic write-downs of 2020 and 2021. But equally a starburst of expansion that will be felt long after Covid subsides.

That's all the positive stuff.

The good, the bad and the ugly

There is, of course, the dense shadow thrown by Covid over so many businesses, from shops to gyms to pubs and hotels, which may never be completely eradicated: the loss of so many businesses that simply couldn't survive. On the high street, as I write, shutters are down, tills are quiet. In terms of retail, the pandemic indelibly altered the world we will be working in – structurally and emotionally. We'll be returning to hollowed-out high streets. More than 17,500 chain stores shut in 2020 – that's forty-eight closures a day – and we haven't seen anything yet. This figure doesn't include the shops that 'temporarily closed' during lockdowns and are unlikely to return.

And for all the small businesses that pivoted, there were many that were simply unable to. The woman running a small catering business. The family outfit running on tight margins that just couldn't make ends meet with no income. We will have lost countless small companies that didn't do anything wrong. They just couldn't survive the catastrophic seizing up of the economy.

Many were businesses that people had put their heart and soul into but simply couldn't weather the storm. Every individual job lost is terrible – the human cost of all this cannot be ignored.

How many ad-hoc signs did we all read on battered bits of A4 stuck in shop windows up and down the country? 'We've had to close up due to Covid restrictions but we look forward to seeing you as soon as we reopen. Until then, keep healthy, keep safe and keep smiling.'

The warmth of the message was underpinned by desperation in many cases. Variations on this theme, hurriedly printed off as the last lockdown announcement came through and the managers closed up, were everywhere. They signalled a world of difficulties for business owners – staffing levels, cashflow problems, ever-changing regulations, supply issues, customer nervousness. Retail – and hospitality – might be the sectors most visibly shuttered, but there isn't an industry that hasn't been affected. Workers confined to desks at home, factories dealing with an onslaught of new and shifting rules, supply chains disrupted, fewer pounds in everyone's pocket. Every organization has learned the hard way the necessity of adapting quickly to a hostile environment.

But for all the great businesses out there who have suffered, we've also lost some for whom the time had come to go. I have to be honest and say that I didn't mourn all the businesses we lost.

In the midst of the pandemic, I was on a radio show talking about the retail market when a friend of mine texted me while I was on air.

'It's about time that someone said that the demise of some of the substance-less brands of the high street is not a bad thing,' she wrote. 'Jobs aside, how did we end up praising these businesses that stole other people's ideas, were terrible for the planet, used slave labour to make the stuff and usually just made one unpleasant fat white man extraordinarily rich?'

Harsh. But true. Too many businesses for too long made

a lot of money for a lot of people at the top, but didn't do much for their employees, didn't do anything for society, didn't attempt to give joy to the individual.

In retail, the cracks were visible for some time: there was a plethora of problems, from decreasing footfall and empty units to punitive business rates. Many giants of the high street paid too much attention to the physics of retail – how fast, how big, how cheap – and not enough to the chemistry – how to engage with their customers. This is what needed to change.

There is something invigorating about this levelling. Just as greenery flourishes again after earth is scorched, so the loss creates space for new businesses to thrive. The co-founder of Lush cosmetics, Mark Constantine, called it 'the Covid rinse'. 'All businesses are having to re-evaluate,' he told me. 'And as they re-evaluate, so the things that are more important to me – climate, the environment, nature – are becoming more important to everyone. Because they know that if they ignore it, they are not going to be successful.'

So how does he see the future? 'I see a vibrant jungle of activity with things we'll be delighted with and things we'll be appalled with. And hopefully we'll be a bit more delighted in the next ten years than in the last.'

The plastic hours

Remember the early days of the pandemic? The time when we all cheerily believed that things would get back to normal quickly? The innocent belief that after a month or maybe three we'd simply switch life back on again lingered for months.

But slowly, our collective mindset shifted as we realized that perhaps it wouldn't be that simple. Now it's a certainty that scars will be left by the past year. From delayed court hearings to postponed operations, from lost education to people who were on the edge and slipped down a crevice into a very dark place, we will be repairing for many years to come.

Mentally and emotionally we now know there will be no normal as we knew it. We can't turn back the clock. Customers are now different. They are not thinking and behaving in the same way as previously. There is a shift in the way they are buying, because there is a shift in the way they are living and seeing the world.

All this means that when we finally, and completely, unshutter it may well be as daunting for many businesses as the lockdowns were. They will have to find new ways to communicate and interact, adapt to massive changes in behaviour and priorities.

But from here on out, the Covid conscience means that brands have to assume they are speaking to a customer – not just a consumer – who is far more conscious of our interconnection than ever. Each breath we took during the pandemic had the potential to infect another. We now understand that we are all intrinsically linked in a way we simply didn't get before. And whether subconsciously, or mindfully, this new mindset has seeped into every part of our lives and affects where we decide to put our money.

Selling to people is becoming about feeding their lives in a better way. There's a whole new level of expectation that the process feeds humanity and the planet too, and while the exact shape of the future is uncertain, what we need to do now is prime ourselves to be as reactive and intuitive as we can be.

As the shuttered high street opens again, there are two ways businesses can go. They can try to hold on to the old ways and aim for high turnover, high profit and nothing else. They can keep the shelves piled high with products with no regard to what resources are being drained. Landlords can just keep bringing in the next business that can afford the shop space, with no regard for how they fit into the local eco-system.

But if we embrace the new landscape, look for a new model that considers real human needs and the society that feeds us, then we could be looking at a whole new horizon. The quantity of shops may go down but the quality will go up.

If this sounds like a rallying cry then that's because it is. This is our moment to create change. Philosopher Gershom Scholem called them 'the plastic hours' – those rare times in history when things align to make deep change possible. He called them 'the crucial moments when it is possible to act. If you move then, something happens.'

As the physicist Carlo Rovelli observes in *The Order of Time*, disorder is not a mistake, it is our default setting. A world in which nothing breaks or fails would be a world with-out innovation or creativity. Or as Jacqueline Novogratz – an inspiring writer and entrepreneur whose mission is to address global poverty – puts it: 'Discomfort is a proxy for progress.'

We are in those plastic hours now. A new future is just there, within our grasp. We just have to grab it. Change has swept through us all. Discomfort is all around. Everyone has a different experience of the last year, of course. And some experiences are more severe than others, often tragically. There is nobody whose life has not been touched. Nobody whose life is not in flux, to some degree or another.

It is up to all of us, then – as organizations, as businesses, as individuals – to take these plastic hours and make some-thing of them. This is why it is important to act now and act well to create businesses that are commercially future-proofed, and that will contribute to true change. Our ability to adapt is a beautiful thing. We mustn't underestimate the power of what we have the potential to achieve.

There will be a new day. The sun will rise. I hope by the time you read this we are all out in the world again. It remains to be seen whether people react to this by going out and splurging, or whether restraint rules the day. But while there will be plenty to mourn in the business landscape, and we can rail, bemoan and cling to what was there before, we can also look at the many possibilities of this opportunity.

Things break down and rebuild again. We need to mourn. We need to feel the fear of this new horizon we are staring at. But we also need to dig into our creativity and rally. We have to put the energy in so that we can build something new.

TO DO
Open Up

For most of us, the first tendency when going through trauma is to close down, look inwards, try to conserve energy and become small. I think we all have felt the pull of that natural instinct when things get tough.

I've discovered, though, that the thing that has helped me get through the last difficult year has been to do the opposite; to draw on as many disparate influences as possible. I have loved the different perspectives that each new discovery brings, which is why I've made them a key part of our weekly newsletter.

Above all, I want to encourage you to ingrain the habit of looking out for new influences so that it comes automatically in hard times. Switch things up: if you usually get your opinion fix from social media, try podcasts instead. If non-fiction is your normal thing, try poetry for a change. Open up; step outside yourself; try something new.

With that in mind, here are some of the things that have helped me through tough times. Some are serious, some are light, some are fleeting and some have dug in and really changed my point of view.

To make you think:

● *Thinking in Systems* by Donella H. Meadows. A book to help you look at problem-solving in a completely new way.

● *On Being* with Krista Tippett. An always energizing podcast that tackles the big questions with an awe-inspiring variety of interviewees.

- *Reality Is Not What It Seems* by Carlo Rovelli. Quantum physics in a can: a book to make you reconsider the whole universe.

- *Can't Get You Out of My Head*. A dazzling, mind-opening documentary series by Adam Curtis.

To make you feel:

- *My Octopus Teacher*. A documentary about a man and an octopus – filled with emotional treasure.

- *GABA* podcast. Meditation, supercharged.

- *Gratitude* by Oliver Sacks. The beautiful last set of essays from an extraordinary mind.

- *The Untethered Soul: The Journey Beyond Yourself* by Michael Singer. Spiritual teachings for a deep view of yourself.

- *A Thousand Mornings* by Mary Oliver. Poems for the big moments and small.

To make you laugh:

- *A Bus Pass Named Desire* by Christopher Matthew. A book of totes hilarious poetry.

- *Kids Write Jokes*. A Twitter compendium of absolutely nonsensical jokes written by children.

- @loveofhuns. Instagram account to make you smile (u ok hun?).

To pull you through:

- *Ten Percent Happier* with Dan Harris. A galvanizing podcast, exploring happiness through meditation and beyond.

- 'You Can't Have It All' by Barbara Ras. An exquisite poem revealing all the things we can have, even if we can't have it all.

- *What Matters Most: Living a More Considered Life* by James Hollis. Answering the huge questions, a Jungian approach to finding your own way.

To give you hope:

- *The Diving-Bell and the Butterfly* by Jean-Dominique Bauby. An absolutely beautiful memoir, never fails to make me weep.

- 'Small Kindnesses' by Danusha Laméris. A poem of quiet celebration.

- *Little Dieter Needs to Fly*: A survival story that encompasses the deepest truths.

3

There Is No 'Us' and 'Them'

Who is this book for?

The short answer to this question is: everyone. But let's break it down into two key groups: people who own and work in businesses and people who buy from them. It's that simple. We're all in this together if we're really going to create exciting, transformative, positive change. We all live in this world, and it has to work for us all.

It might be tempting to sit back and say, 'Everything you are talking about, all the flaws and the untrammelled growth and the bad practices that result from that is just the way the system is. The world is always going to turn this way, and businesses have to play on the field they're put on.'

Of course, we know that the businesses that have focused only on growth have often been highly successful. There will still be businesses doing the same sort of thing moving forward. But because the world is changing, there will be less room for that kind of company, that kind of brand, because there are fewer people happy to do business with them.

If you're in business, you can keep going down that route, act only in your own interests and make a quick buck. You'll probably even do OK for a while. But here's the thing: you won't be able to do it indefinitely. In the retail sphere, the companies that have followed this model are crashing down around us. Goodbye, Topshop. And while there are always younger businesses ready to fill their shoes – hello, Boohoo – history tells us that somehow, sometime, they may well be a victim of their own individual brand of financial success.

Whether the people raking it in right now will care, I don't know. But *we* will care. And *you* will care because you're reading this book. I truly believe that most businesses do care, and that is why so many brilliant business people are developing brands and companies that prioritize social progress as well as the bottom line, brands that attract conscious buyers rather than passive consumers, that seek out ways to put something back in. They are part of a whole new, better way of doing business. They are keeping an eye on the longer game, building healthy businesses that give back and can endure and add to how we live, instead of just taking. Businesses rooted in the Kindness Economy. Businesses that know that to work, they have to work for all of us.

Finding our voice

I became aware of a really profound shift in the way we buy and sell a decade ago, when it impacted on retail and the high street. I couldn't put that feeling into words as I can now, but I knew instinctively that the old way of doing things was simply no longer serving us – it wasn't sustainable. Aside from the livelihoods being affected by the slow erosion of the high street, I could see the wider picture of our increased dislocation and loneliness.

So when I was commissioned by the government to look into the state of the high street (because in many places they'd become desolate places, populated by bookies and badly run charity shops), I knew almost before I started what recommendations the Portas Review would give on how to reimagine them and enable them to thrive.

The 'success' story that everyone banged on about was the shift to out-of-town retail parks, to which supermarkets and chain stores selling everything from clothes to toys and pet food were moving. The rent was cheaper. Their profit margins improved. This was what success looked like and more and more of these grey industrial drive-ins were springing up.

As every successive minister in charge turned up to give their opinion (the responsibility changed hands five times during the period I worked on the report), I seemed to have the same conversation over again: surely, they all said, wide-eyed, these joyless parks were what people wanted – that was what accounted for their success. If I was in the room with any of them now, I'd be far more vocal about telling them where to shove that particular pearl of wisdom. Did they seriously think that people dreamed of driving to a bland retail park on the edge of town?

People didn't want to do that. They did that because high streets were being eroded and this was often all that was on offer. We were all plugged into the consumerist matrix and just went wherever the best BOGOF was to be found. If you move all the energy out of the high streets, it stands to reason nobody will visit them. But where was the people's voice in all this? Who actually asked them?

It's time to reclaim our voice, to fully embrace the idea that every pound we spend is a vote for how we want to live.

Think about that sentence, embrace it and feel its power. In a world where most of us feel increasingly meaningless in the face of big tech, computerized systems and governments that seem as remote as the court of Louis XIV did to the peasants of seventeenth-century France, the sense of our own individual power has been sapped away.

But by spending wisely, with companies that reflect your values, you can reclaim it. And together we can create the kind of critical mass needed to bring the Kindness Economy fully to life.

I really want all of us to take this on board: it's time to abandon the chicken and egg of whether businesses drive values – or if we as consumers do. They're interdependent, we'll never pull them apart. Which means that if every one of us takes up the mantle of conscious consumerism, rather than mindless consumption, we can create change on a huge level.

The good news is that more and more of us are not only realizing that we hold this power, we are willing to use it.

The pandemic only accelerated this tendency. It helped erode the idea of businesses as operating apart from the rest of us. On a local level, you could see it everywhere as pet shops, restaurants and everything in between started delivering straight to their people. Suddenly, we all saw how impoverished our lives would be if these businesses didn't survive and so we got behind them. The idea of the collective 'we' trounced the individualist 'me'. It was no longer about siloed individual organizations. This was about all of us.

The furore over the food provided to home-schooled pupils was a case in point. In January 2021, as the country hunkered down into the third bout of lockdown in a year, pictures of sad-looking ingredients laid out on tables started to flood social media: half a pepper wrapped in cling film, two carrots, a loaf of bread, a tin of beans and three potatoes.

This was the result of the government scrapping the voucher scheme for home-schooling pupils on free school meals, handing contracts to a catering company to provide food parcels instead. But these sad-looking scraps were replacing what should have been a £30 voucher to last a child a week. Something was really wrong.

Campaigners, led by the footballer Marcus Rashford (who had already, just six months before, forced the government to reverse their decision not to provide free school meals for children over half-term), got out their calculators and their shopping receipts and started shouting like crazy.

They looked at how far they themselves could stretch £30 in the average supermarket (even without the benefit of a bulk order discount), calculated the margins, asked questions about the salaries of the top dogs in the company, and came to the conclusion that the whole thing was a triumph of profit over doing what was right.

At first, the government's response was predictably tepid. When Chartwells, the catering company involved, said the food boxes had 'fallen short in this instance', the government said they were looking into it. But within days, as more and more pictures of inadequate and unhealthy food parcels filtered out into the public consciousness, the government went back to the voucher scheme. Victory for the grass-roots campaigners. Imagine how much better this would have been if the government had let local businesses provide food to their local schools. Not only could money have been kept in the local economy, but they could have avoided the faceless, unaccountable behaviour from a big corporation. It takes connection and community to care.

In the same way, consumers and employees are having their say in the business sphere: whether it's Uber drivers using the legal system to change the entire employment model of the company or US shoppers boycotting the brands and stores that didn't meaningfully support the BLM movement.

It's no longer a question of 'them upstairs' running

things, and us down here grumbling that it's all a bit crap but letting them get on with it. Now there is a new feeling. If politics is letting us down, is there a better way?

We talk a lot about the downsides of social media. But isn't this increased sense of a voice that so many people feel they have on social platforms also exciting? It gives us all a way to shape the future as consumers. And for businesses, it offers opportunities to connect in new ways with our customers, to forge a bond that goes far deeper than simply supplying them goods. It offers opportunities for innovation and ideas, to discover what our customers really want and how we can give it to them.

The power of 'we'

All of this might feel a bit frightening for businesses (nobody likes being shouted at, even if it is over the internet), but the rewards can be massive.

James Watt is a hugely successful businessman. In 2007 he and his business partner Martin Dickie were micro-selling their new beer – two guys filling bottles by hand and selling from the back of a van. Today their company BrewDog is valued at about $2 billion and is the only carbon negative brewing company in the world.

Right from the start, BrewDog was built on the principle of listening to its customers. More than that, their 'Equity for Punks' scheme, which they started two years into their business journey, has built a community of customers that actually owns 20 per cent of the brand.

It isn't just about investment. They want to 'shorten the distance between ourselves and the people who enjoy the beers that we make'.

Listen to how James described this community to me: 'They're not investors. They're advocates. They're ambassadors. They're our biggest fans. They're our harshest critics. They help us find new locations. They help us develop new beers. They are very much on this journey with us.'

There are currently 180,000 members of this community, a community which has raised £85 million – the largest sum raised by crowdfunding anywhere in the world to date.

But for James and his colleagues, it's not about the money raised. 'It's about what we can do with this fantastic community – who believe what we believe, who are passionate about what we are passionate about, who believe in investing in our people, who believe in looking after our planet, who believe in trying to change the world of beer through passion and integrity.'

James believes that in the future who we spend our money with will be more important than who we vote for. So now, more than ever, we must each take ownership of where our future is going.

Whether you buy, whether you sell, whether you create or whether you consume. If you're in a business; if you own a business, big or small; if you're part of a business; or if you buy from that business, you can contribute. Because all of these things are the way we make choices.

And that starts with the money in our pockets.

TO DO

Ask yourself some questions

Every pound spent is a vote for the kind of society we want to live in. We are not passive: we all have agency in the world, perhaps more than we think. That's the great news. But as we all know – with great power comes great responsibility. How to exercise this agency we hold?

Start by asking questions.

The first question is about yourself: **'What are the faces I present to the world?'** None of us is just one identity. We all wear more than one hat: we may be business people, but we may also be parents, or children, or neighbours, or leaders in our community. We may be selling things, but we also buy. We have influence as much as we are influenced by others. Which leads to the second question: **'Am I able to bring my personal values into each of these identities? If not, why not?'**

With that initial thought, under those hats of ours, we can turn our attention outwards and bring that questioning spirit to all the different aspects of our lives:

• *When we buy*: **'Where am I putting my money? Could it be better spent elsewhere?'** Do the places where you spend your money reflect how you want to live your life? Don't limit this to the obvious – the money you hand over at the till. It also applies to the background spending of every corner of your life: the bank that houses your money; where your pension fund is invested; your energy provider. All these everyday decisions build to make a difference.

● *When we work*: **'Am I happy with my work?'** Does it align with your own personal values? Are you able to bring your best self into your work or do you have to leave it at the door?

    'Where in my organization can I use my voice?' Are you given the opportunity to have your say? What can you use that voice for?

    Above all, are you able to be authentic to your true self? Ask yourself: **'Am I behaving as a "business person", or as a *person*?'**

● *When we build businesses*: **'What is my organization bringing to the world?'** As a business builder there's a very clear sense of our impact on the world around us, from the services and goods we provide, to the networks of suppliers and clients we are hooked into, to the people we employ. What is your business's impact on these circles of influence?

Beyond this, our businesses sit within a community, and within the wider world. **'Are we having a positive impact? What are we bringing to the conversation? What** values do we embody? What boundaries are we pushing forward?'

● *When we parent*: You are bringing up the next generation of consumers, activists, voters, citizens. **'What can I tell them about what to value in the world and how to show up? What are my actions showing them?'**

● *When we go online*: Like it or not, the conversations (arguments) that rage online shape the world. Let's not be one personality in the streets, and another in the tweets. How you show up in the online space matters. **'What is my online presence putting out into the world? Would I stand behind it in real life?'**

You won't have the perfect answer to all of these questions. None of us do. We ask the questions because they open the paths to self-discovery, and, through that, to finding our voice and having our say.

4

The New Principles

Swift's Hill is a place I have come to love. In recent years, I've walked this hidden corner of the beautifully wild Gloucestershire countryside under grey skies and blue, during the pared-back simplicity of winter and the burgeoning wildflower carpet of spring. It's the place, particularly during the turbulent times of the Covid lockdowns, where I go to clear my head and reconnect to the simple rhythms of nature.

My children also share my love of Swift's Hill. And on this particular day, I'm striding upwards with my son Mylo. We've been in a bubble together during the pandemic and, as ever, conversations are lively around the dinner table. My children certainly inherited my love of discussion.

Both Mylo and my daughter Verity are very much their own people, but it's sure they've also been impacted by my attitudes. And they represent the two different sides to me: while Verity's career is values-driven and her ambition centres on environmental issues, Mylo is more commercially minded. He likes the cut and thrust of business, the personal drive and growth and, yes, he likes to make some money. Just like I do.

'So how are you going to convince people to believe in the Kindness Economy?' says Mylo as we head towards the top of Swift's Hill.

'Because it's about doing the right thing,' I reply. 'It's pretty simple really.'

He looks at me in that particularly withering way that only your children can.

'Yes, I agree,' he says. 'But how do you get Joe to go and work at Company A, which is doing the right thing, but where he'll probably earn less than Sam, who's at Company B that's all about maximizing profit so he'll make more? I'm sure Joe would like to do the right thing, but he also wants a nice life.'

And this, dear reader, is my son's ninja skill: cutting the crap. We talk and the rest of the conversation I'll leave on the hill.

But Mylo's question is important, and I need to answer it because it's true that people have to be convinced to go on this journey if we're really going to create change.

Going back to basics: let me be clear that there's nothing wrong with making money. The Kindness Economy isn't some anti-capitalism esoteric theory. Profit is certainly not inherently bad – it drives entrepreneurship, contributes to society through tax, encourages investment. We all need a certain amount of money, first to survive, and then to thrive, at least materialistically – and if a lovely holiday or decent wine is materialistic, then I'm a paid-up member of that club.

It's the way you create profit, however, the maximizing of it at any cost, that can become problematic. If profit is all that matters, and screw the impact of creating it, then that's where the questions must start.

There are of course jobs that pay better, and jobs that pay worse. And, sadly, the ones that do good for people or planet – from saving whales to teaching our kids – tend to pay worse. We just don't value these things financially. (Don't get me started on just how undervalued all the unpaid caring work that women mostly do is.) On the other side of the coin are the jobs that are all about making money – by selling stuff, services or resources – and these tend to pay better. Money values money.

(Another point here is that even if you're in a job that pays better, it's often the people at the top of the pile who are really making the money. Sam might be making more than Joe but it's Peter on the board who's coining it in. Just look at the 940 per cent increase in CEO compensation over the past forty years. Top bosses now earn 117 times the annual pay of the average worker.)

But going back to making profit, it ain't what you do – it's the way that you do it.

If you find that in the pursuit of making money you are damaging the wellbeing of society, the people who work for you, the planet and even your own health, then you've got to question it. Believe in profit. Believe in creating. Believe in building. Believe in success. Just not at the cost of the world and humanity.

For me, it comes down to a simple matter of principle: the give-a-fucks and the don't-give-a-fucks.

The latter are businesses motivated purely on price and screw the consequences. Hello to the purveyors of the super-cheap Black Friday dress and the highly digitized, transactional and impersonal peak predators of tomorrow's retail. It's treating people like animals: is that really OK?

The former are the businesses who are either doing the right thing – or who want to, but just haven't worked out exactly how yet. And together they can create a critical mass that will drive true change.

The shift isn't about ripping up your business plans and turning your back on profit. It's about looking at the bigger picture to see what it is that is going to make your business work in a new landscape.

There's also a commercial reality to this. Right now, 77 per cent of people globally say they value decency in business as much as price and convenience. This figure is only going to increase. So the question isn't whether you should get on board with this change – it's hurtling down the barrel at us, like it or not – it's when. And the answer is now.

The Kindness Economy

In December 2019 – remember those days, before the pandemic hit us? – I stood on stage in London to give a TED talk. It was invigorating – a fantastic opportunity to articulate everything I had been working on for the previous years under one simple banner: the Kindness Economy.

For me, this was a coming together of so many different streams. There was the gradual realization of the toll my industry had taken on the world, and a recognition of the part I had played in that. There was all the research I had done for my book *Work Like a Woman* – which had taught me the immense value of female power in business, but also that there was much more to say and much more to be done if we want to change the norms by which businesses operate. There were the conversations I'd had with so many inspiring people for my *WLAW* podcasts. There were the changes I was putting into place in my own business – a journey of discovery that could be challenging but which was daily opening up my eyes to a new way of working. All of this was feeding a blindingly clear revelation: everything has to change. And here I was, bringing it all together under the eyes of the TED cameras and a fantastic audience.

At the heart of the talk, at the heart of all the work my team and I have done on this, was one basic realization. For us, it starts with people.

The Kindness Economy is about: People. Planet. Profit. In that order. Sustainability issues have taken centre stage in the global conversation; understandably so given the drumbeat of urgency that surrounds them. But, by focusing on the planet, we risk leaving something even more important out of the equation: humanity. The problem we have is broader than just the planet. This is a symbiosis: what is in the planet's interest is in humanity's interest, and vice versa. We need to put people at the centre, because it is people who will make the change.

That TED talk was just the start – it led to columns in newspapers, to grass-roots discussions with businesses. Throughout the dark days of the pandemic, the work I had done on the Kindness Economy was guiding my footsteps. It led us to putting together the Kindness Economy Report, aimed at helping businesses to reset their thinking. It inspired me into a new podcast series – called (you've guessed it) *The Kindness Economy*. All the interviewees I spoke to – brilliant economists, business leaders, bankers, architects – were turning their considerable brainpower to thinking about how to build a different and better tomorrow. Every conversation opened my eyes to a different avenue to pursue. It was exhilarating.

What I was trying to do through all of this was map out a new set of principles; principles that successful businesses could use to build themselves into forces for good. If we have to moderate growth – and we do – then what are we putting in its place? How will we judge ourselves, as individuals, as organizations, if we make growth and profit only part of the equation? This is going to be a whole new territory: what are the waymarkers going to be? The fundamental question is this: how can you build a business that marries commercial success with the basic human principles of decency and compassion?

Well, for a start you should want your business to do *more* than just grow.

The economist Manfred Max-Neef tells us that, 'Growth is a quantitative accumulation, development is the liberation of creative possibilities. Every living system in nature grows up to a certain point and stops growing. As a person it comes to a point when you stop growing, but you continue to develop yourself. Development has no limits.'

It's time to pivot our core goal from growing to developing but also thriving. Thriving is something different to mere growth. Growth for growth's sake is unthinking and insatiable – it takes up space, extracts from its surroundings, mutates itself and whatever lies in its path. It measures our worth by way of 'productivity'. (It also seems to have crept its way into many a marketer's title these past few years – I predict that'll reverse before too long . . .).

In the online 'crypto community' there's a mantra that is doing the rounds: 'Up only'. This dedicated focus on vertical growth is illusory (and impossible). It reminds me of the analogy drawn by the psychologist Andrew Solomon in his book on parenting diverse children, *Far from the Tree: Parents, Children and the Search for Identity*. He distinguishes between vertical identity, which is directly inherited, and horizontal identity, which is drawn from our peers, our environment – a richer seam, perhaps. It's the difference between looking in all directions rather than being fixed on a straight line.

Thriving means healthy, balanced, resilient, regenerative.

It means a business has roots that are nourished by the good soil they are planted in and contribute to the surrounding ecosystem in a lasting way. It measures our worth by way of motivation, wellbeing and impact. It's a beautiful word, used to describe humanity at its best. Precisely why we should apply it to business.

Thriving allows space – within the parameters of business success – for kindness to flourish.

The 'ands'

So what does a thriving business in the Kindness Economy look like? Well, let me reassure you right now – it's not perfect. I could give you a long list of all the things 'good' businesses absolutely need to do and be. But that's not the Kindness Economy – that's the Righteous Economy. And, as we know only too well, nothing is that black and white. Or if it is, it leads us nowhere. New Year's resolutions to be the best, fittest, nicest, cleverest person ever, anyone? Precisely.

What I will give you is a series of fundamental, evolutionary shifts that will start the momentum we need to get us moving, at pace, in the right direction. From the way we all think, to the way we buy, sell, work and live. They're all relevant because they all work together to create change.

Growth Economy	Kindness Economy
Me Me Me	Me AND We
Siloed Businesses	Internal AND External Interconnectedness
Value for Money	Values AND Value (the Double V)
Serving Customers	Serving Customers AND the Community
Data	Data AND Creative Instinct
Passive Consumers	People Consciously Buying AND Living
Buying From	Buying From AND Buying Into
Material Comfort	Human Dignity AND Material Comfort
Financial Growth	Social AND Financial Impact
Hindsight/Rear-view Mirror Analysis	Hindsight AND Foresight
Disruption	Disruption AND Reimagination
Reduce Impact	Reduce Impact AND Add More
Hard Skills	Hard AND Soft Skills
Short Term	Long Term AND Short Term
Famous for Saying	Famous for Doing AND Saying – Role Model Culture

You'll notice on the right-hand side of this table a recurring word: 'AND'. That's no coincidence. One of my favourites, the Sufi poet Rumi, once wrote: 'You think because you understand "one" you must also understand "two", because one and one make two. But you must also understand "and".'

How very true. And profound. But also deeply practical. I'll explain. The 'and' represents the real business world, the one we occupy and contend with day to day. Nothing, including business, is black and white. We must set standards, yes, but we have to ensure that those standards are possible. There is no point having a beautiful vision if your company can't break even.

At Portas, we spend a lot of time working with businesses who are wrestling with changing the engines while flying the plane . . . while transforming into a phoenix. Hell, we are one of those businesses ourselves. So we look at the numbers, but we prioritize creativity alongside them. We think in the long term, but that doesn't mean we let go of our short-term targets. We embrace and champion the collective 'we', of course, but we also recognize the individual 'me' too – because it's human nature to want to better things for yourself and your own.

Remember, right at its core, the Kindness Economy asks that we hold at the heart all three things: People, Planet, Profit. In that order.

Buying into, not just buying from

Some of the shifts on this list are relatively simple; some are complex enough that they warrant a whole chapter. At this point, I want to pick out just a few. What, for instance, do I mean by the shift from passive consumers to active buyers?

Think of it like this: the way we buy is a reflection of how we live. Whether we like it or not, the choices we make about how we spend our money – or don't spend our money – are intimately bound up in our identities. Status, and how we are seen in the eyes of others, is something that is central to most humans. It's ingrained. It's in all our choices: where we live, what we eat, what we wear, what car we drive. And businesses know this, so one of the things that businesses are selling is status.

When I started out in the eighties, it was all about status symbols. About the brand. Were you driving a Porsche? Had you got the right trainers? Did your sunglasses have the right logo on them? You wore your status. It was overt, in-your-face. It was aspiration, yuppies, *The Wolf of Wall Street*. Donald Trump with bundles of cash on the cover of *People* magazine. You showed your wealth. You flaunted it. You had made it.

But then the picture shifted. Where once luxury had just been for the people at the top of the tree, suddenly the masses were in on it. The actor Danniella Westbrook head to toe in Burberry check, pushing a Burberry buggy with a matching baby inside. Burberry all over the football terraces. And suddenly it all felt a bit gauche; labels had lost their cachet for the fashion leader crowd.

So we moved into a phase of status stories. It wasn't just about the big labels any more. Instead, it was about seeking out what was special, and having the knowledge and the insight to know what the 'right thing' was. It was all about the bag by this exclusive designer you'd discovered in the Marais. You weren't buying perfumes from the department store counter so much as a bespoke scent crafted by a small boutique perfumery someone had told you about. You were in the know. The dress you were wearing? 'Oh, it comes from a tiny women's collective in Nepal, darling.'

This was particularly rife in the world of food – you'd be 'sourcing' your dinner party fare from a particular farmer in the Welsh hills, or a smokery in the Outer Hebrides. Even the supermarkets were making sure they put a picture of an appropriately weathered farmer on the front of their packaging.

So it was all much less brash and much more subtle, but it was still about status, and we were still buying stuff. We weren't at the stage of realizing that we were screwing the planet. That we were screwing ourselves.

But now, finally, we are recognizing that we buy too much – and that this is not a good thing.

Plastics were one of the first big signifiers: think of the loss of status involved if you were to see me coming out of the supermarket loaded up with disposable plastic bags. What would it signal about me? It would signal that I am just not thinking. That I am not reusing, recycling, or caring about my impact on the planet. That my values are not right.

Nowadays we want how we spend our money to reflect the fact that we do care, that we are responsible, that we are thinking about the issues involved, that we are conscious and conscientious.

Instead of an armful of disposable plastic, I would probably want to tell you how I have found the most wonderful woman who makes specially woven, sustainably sourced bags for life, and she's a small business and works from a shed at the end of the garden which is powered only by solar panels. And I'll probably go on to tell you how I try to shop locally and support the wonderful butcher down the road and don't waste petrol driving to the supermarket. All of these things will be signals of the kind of person I want to be: someone who wants to do good.

I joke a little, but this desire is deeply held, and getting more so. The majority (51 per cent) of Gen Z research a brand's corporate social responsibility (CSR) practices before buying. It's a turn in the tide of consumer behaviour that will never be reversed.

What we are entering now is the time of status sentience – sentience signifying feeling, intuitive understanding. We will spend our money with businesses that demonstrate to us that they care: that they respect our planet and our communities and our people. This goes not just for the old status signifiers of cars and clothing and homeware. Now we are conscious also about what electricity companies we use and who we bank with, even who we get our loo paper from. What we require from the businesses we interact with now is that they put something back in. People actively want brands to help drive change.

- 58 per cent of people say they want brands to be a positive force in shaping culture, according to a global poll in 2020.

- 61 per cent would like them to work towards making the future better than the present.

- 57 per cent are more likely to buy from brands that support their community.

- 55 per cent – more than half of UK shoppers – now consider the impact of clothing production on the environment to be 'severe', up from 35 per cent in 2017.

Today more and more of us are aware of what all this consumption is costing us and, crucially for anyone in business, this awareness is driving how people buy. This is the difference between buying *from*, and buying *into*. Customers want to buy from brands whose values reflect their own. This doesn't just apply to show-off, high-end purchases. For the new generation coming through, this principle sits across all goods. We don't want the way we spend our money to be merely transactional.

Let's not get too comfortable, though; we may be conscious about this stuff, but we should also be aware that being conscious isn't enough, and there's still a bloody long way to go. Time is of the essence, and we don't have much of it left to repair the damage that has already been done.

We're certainly at a point where there's a lot of virtue signalling going on. Some businesses are doing surface-deep 'good' things and then contradicting them deeper inside their processes. But moving forward, as people become ever more aware, these values will not be easily faked. They need to thread right through the company structure. They need to be real.

We know we can no longer afford a business world built on the principles of greed and gain. We know that a focus on the bottom line is no longer enough. Now, we need to be guided into the right direction by a new compass. One that is set by good ideas. New ideas. A new model, which is about kindness and the economy. We want businesses to work. It's just that we want them to work for us too. Each business, however big or small, must play its part in lifting people and planet, not damaging both. What is the ultimate good to any of us if profits increase, if growth is rampant, but the world itself is in a downwards spiral?

The long and the short of it

There's no doubt we are in an age characterized by relentless, butterfly-minded, speeded-up thinking.

As Stewart Brand, founder of the Long Now Foundation, describes: 'Civilization is revving itself into a pathologically short attention span. Some sort of balancing corrective to the short-sightedness is needed, some mechanism or myth that encourages the long view and the taking of long-term responsibility . . .'

In the same way, the philosopher Roman Krznaric points to a need for 'cathedral thinking' – the necessity for us to project our mindset beyond a single lifespan, to undertake projects beyond the scope of our immediate benefit.

To build a business with values that are truly worthwhile, you need to fix your eyes on a horizon longer than the quarterly figures. But let's be realistic; you need to think also about the short-term goals. Bluntly, you will never build your cathedral for tomorrow if you don't have enough cashflow to pay your stonemasons today. The Kindness Economy requires us to keep our eye on both frameworks – short and long.

As Daniel Kahneman pointed out in *Thinking, Fast and Slow*, humans are good at the intuitive, immediate, instinctive kind of thinking. It's harder to tease out the long-term, rational approach. Harder, but necessary, if we are to make lasting change.

But these are uncertain times: how to think long term when we don't even know what the next year will bring? What if your long-term vision is simply to stay afloat? Long-termism may sound like something you turn your attention to when times are bountiful: get those short-term goals realized, get the profits piling up, and then you can turn your attention to a grander purpose. Sounds logical, but no. This stuff needs to be baked into the bones of an organization.

It's a fallacy to say that in tough times broader thinking isn't a priority – or, worse, represents a cost. For a historical example, look to the great Quaker businesses of the nineteenth century. Cadbury's, Fry's, Lloyds, Clarks, Barclays. All household names to this day, and built on values which encompassed real long-term thinking – the need for community, for housing, for education. 'The real goal of an employer is to seek for others the best life of which they are capable,' said Joseph Cadbury. Hear, hear.

The philanthropical vision of these companies is well known – more surprising is the fact that these businesses were built at a time of recession. These were tough businessmen operating in a hard market. Survival for them was part of their social responsibility – a means to ensure that the values they drove through their organizations would endure. Their values were not 'costs' that fought against the viability of the business. They were an integral part. Indeed, you might argue, as historian Deborah Cadbury does, that it was when they let go of the Quaker values at their heart that these businesses became vulnerable to decline and takeover.

The power of our example

'We lead not by the example of our power, but by the power of our example': the words of the new President of the USA, Joe Biden, on his inauguration in January 2021.

The final entry on the list, 'Famous for doing AND saying', may surprise you. But this is a key signifier of where a society puts its energy. The kinds of people we collectively look up to as role models is a significant tell as to the values we celebrate. We'll always have role models, but I've noticed that the criteria for who we choose to look up to are changing: we're moving from idolizing the trifecta of Power, Fame and Money to something more interesting.

Think about footballers: it used to be that the footballer who crossed most thoroughly into the non-football-fan consciousness was David Beckham. Why? Because he *had* a lot of stuff. Now? I would say the crown at the moment goes to Marcus Rashford. Because he *does* a lot of stuff. It's the difference between Beckham sporting his tats and his quiff in every ad going, and Marcus Rashford campaigning to make real change and celebrating the strength of his mother who brought him up to be proud of his values.

When I started my business, pretty much every brand that came into the agency was determined to be 'iconic'. As a buzzword, it was absolutely everywhere. Now, it feels so dated – I don't think I've heard the word in my office for years. What everyone wants to be today, incidentally, is 'loved'.

There's a difference between icons and role models. Icons are garlanded objects that are set far above us, high up on a plinth somewhere: untouchable, ready for us to worship. Role models are active, they are doing something; marking out a role that we want to follow.

Youth has captured this role model game in a way they never did before: where young people used to be famous as pop stars, actors, football players, now Greta Thunberg, possibly the most famous teenager on the planet, is in that position due to the strength of her beliefs and the fierceness of her actions.

It's the same with Malala Yousafzai. Another girl – a young woman now – changing the world. How great was it back in 2014 to hear my young daughter tell me that, inspired by Malala, her greatest ambition was to win the Nobel Peace Prize? Even models, traditionally the blankest of canvases, have found their voice, with the likes of Adwoa Aboah and Halima Aden using theirs to initiate change. To go back to the Biden inauguration: the president's words were stirring, but the person who really captured hearts was the young poet Amanda Gorman. It's not hard to see that this energy is where the future lies.

Just as our buying habits now prioritize status sentience rather than status symbols, we are using a different set of criteria. The pandemic has heightened this effect. Now we're thinking about what people actually do with their lives and how they contribute. We're looking at the keyworkers, the doctors, the nurses on the front line, and we are in awe. The Banksy painting of a little boy, superhero toys discarded, playing with the caped toy figure of a nurse encapsulates this perfectly – one reason it sold for over £14 million in an auction to benefit the NHS.

The other day my team and I were trying to put together a list of the top fifty icons for the present day. Beyond the first five or six, we began to falter, because everyone's answers became so different. People were as likely to say their mum, or an activist they were following, as some film star or 'influencer'. In the end we couldn't come up with a definitive list – a fact that in itself tells us we're experiencing significant change in what matters to us.

Businesses need to recognize this particular cultural evolution not just as a vehicle for marketing (though it will help you pick the best person to be your brand ambassador), but because it points to a deeper truth about what society values. Reading these runes, understanding what culture is demanding now, is vital.

The 'we' and the 'me'

As with everything else in the Kindness Economy, the fundamental momentum here is the shift from 'me' to 'me and we'.

It's no longer a question of 'me' or 'we'; it's a recognition that these aren't in opposition but need to be in harmony. The interests of the individual are fusing with the interests of society. Especially among millennials and Gen Z, there isn't a division between the two: what is best for the 'we' is best for the 'me' and vice versa. Businesses need to pay attention, because this is increasingly borne out in the attitudes of customers. We are moving from this interconnectedness being a hope, to a desire, to being an expectation. An Edelman Trust survey that spanned eight countries including the US and the UK found that 80 per cent of people want brands to solve societal problems. In the wake of the pandemic 84 per cent want brand social channels to facilitate a feeling of community and offer support to those in need.

The shift here is about a willingness to embrace the changes that will benefit us all.

Talking about what it takes to make a difference, Jacqueline Novogratz comes up with a simple but radical idea: 'What if each of us gave more to the world than we took from it? Everything would change.' She is speaking about each of us as individuals, but it works at a business level also, where businesses too need to think about 'we'. Wouldn't it be great if a business, generationally, could leave the world in a better place than it found it?

If that sounds a bit too utopian, ask yourself this: 'Is there any reason why I can't do this at the same time as being commercial? Why can't the two work together?'

I didn't quite manage to convey all this to Mylo as we

stood at the top of Swift's Hill. But there, my razor-sharp, witty, sometimes infuriating son, is my answer: there will always be Sams in this world who just want the biggest pay-cheque, and there will always be businesses who want the same thing. But if Joe makes a good wage, works for a company that cares and leaves the world a better place, in keeping with his own values, then I believe he'll be a happier man for it.

TO DO
Imagine your future

It's time to imagine a different future. What could your corner of the Kindness Economy look like?

Once upon a time, this might have been the place where I encouraged businesses to start mapping out a five-year plan. But if the Covid year has taught us anything, it would be that that five-year plan isn't worth the pixels it is written with.

Change is daunting. It's easy to get polarized in our thinking: we tend either to have an aversion to change, or to rush headlong and unthinking into the next big thing. Let's think of a different way to go about this.

At Portas, our strategy started with a list. We call it the Change/Unchange list. We sat down and made a note of everything that we do, everything in our environment, everything we embody. Each entry filed under one of two columns: what are the things we absolutely can't – or absolutely won't – change? And what are the things we can, and should?

Start with that. Use the table that contrasts the Growth Economy with the Kindness Economy on page 49. Where are the spaces for you to find your 'ands'?

Some things are going to be specific to your company: Who do you serve? What are your value systems? What makes you you? What are you proud of? What are you passionate about? What is your output? How do you operate? How do you treat your employees? What are your networks?

Some are universal: the business environment you operate in. The ups and downs of the market.

Some are simply the facts of human nature, the things we can sometimes forget when we are doing blue-sky thinking. Some things are hard-wired into us as humans (the need to connect, for instance), and good luck to any business strategy that chooses to ignore them.

Now, what do you want to keep? And what do you want to change? The Kindness Economy doesn't require that you change from a panda to a parrot. This is about adaptive evolution. At Portas, we are changing a lot, but we can only make those changes because we are hanging on to our unchanges. The things that make us us.

The Change/Unchange list works for each of us as individuals, just as it does for businesses. We can use it to examine our lives, not just our working practices. Is there anything about the way we are living that doesn't align with our values? What could we do to change it?

This is the time for ruthless honesty. It's about paring back, a quest to find the base coordinates of who you are. These coordinates will guide every decision you make as you take your place in the Kindness Economy – that isn't daunting: it's empowering.

5

Getting Started

So – that is what the Kindness Economy looks like. Now all we have to do is put it in place. Easy, right?

I know. This stuff sounds daunting. Here you are with a job to do, maybe a business to run. On Monday morning, you're going to have to sit down and look at the numbers. There are financial targets to hit and regulations to comply with, employees to manage. Your days are full. Maybe you're working long days for someone else and running a family too, and, in your world, convenience trumps everything. And now I'm telling you about this gigantic undertaking – nothing less than remodelling the very construct of capitalism and finding your place within it. Where in hell are you meant to start with that? How will it even work?

Breathe. Don't panic. You're reading this book, which means you're interested, open; you're on board with the idea of change and you want to have a conversation. Great news – some of the ideas here are the very first tools you'll need, and you are already using them.

Businesses often make this too huge and monolithic; they think they need to start out by defining some enormous but somehow vague target: 'We need to revolutionize our entire organization along sustainable lines by the end of 2030'; 'We need to redesign our business model along a ten-point plan to prioritize wellbeing.' We do the same as individuals:

'Everything I buy needs to be organic from now on'; 'We as a family should be reducing our waste to practically zero.' All this without quite pinpointing exactly why, or how. It's over-whelming and confusing.

I'm going to give you the first and most simple piece of advice. I wish I could take credit for it, but it's from Pema Chodron, a Buddhist nun and spiritual teacher, who has been a guiding sage in my life.

Anytime that I realize I am letting the world get too much into my head, or I get stressed and start drawing my energy from bad ideas, I go back to her. One of her sayings – the title of one of her books, in fact – really resonates here: 'Start where you are.'

Look inside. Begin with yourself. Not as a 'professional' cogging company targets, but as a human being. It's a simple but powerful reset. Put people, including yourself, first – and change happens.

It starts with you as an individual: 'Am I behaving in a way that is respectful of myself and of others?' So much of what we do is informed by how other people behave. Instead, connect with your inner voice and think about what you know is right. This applies to every part of our lives, not just how we show up in our work. Think of it as a heartbeat that rip-ples outwards, from yourself, through your employees or your colleagues, through your organization, your customers, your community, out into the wider world. Empathy power-ing progress; the steady pulse that sets the rhythm and tone of a whole business.

Partners not suppliers. Relationships not transactions. People not staff, not consumers. Language matters. It has the power to humanize – and dehumanize.

As individuals, as customers, this sense of humanity is

what we should be looking for in the brands and businesses we interact with.

For an example of a company that has truly rippled their values outwards from the centre of their organization into the wider community, look at Timpson, the shoe repair and key-cutting business. A family company that was founded over 150 years ago, it is built around strong principles, ones that sit right at the heart not only of the current CEO James Timpson, but of the whole dynasty. (James's parents fostered over ninety children, which gives you some idea of their family values.)

This is a company that has always believed that the business starts with the people who work for them: 'Our whole business is based on a culture of trust and kindness,' says James. The business operates what it calls 'upside-down management', centring support on the people who they believe need it most: the employees manning the front lines behind the tills.

This means empowering them by giving them authority and agency, and 'trusting them to make decisions as they see fit'. Priding itself on being a good employer, Timpson's culture of putting people first runs through the entire company. They are imaginative with their benefits – from buying a car for a colleague in need, to ensuring that everyone who works for the business can use the company's holiday homes – and serious about being supportive. From hardship funds to generous bonus schemes (on top of the living wage), this is a company that looks after its people. This goes in good times and bad – the pandemic has lost the company £50 million, but they are still ensuring they top up furloughed salaries so that all employees get paid in full.

'I'm as commercial as you get,' says James, 'but I've

learned that if colleagues don't come first, you won't achieve your commercial goals.'

From empowering their employees, the company culture widens out to serving its customers – 'Just say yes' to customers is a company motto, as is 'Amaze your customers' – and beyond: since 2002 the company has had an initiative to employ ex-offenders through its Timpson Foundation, and by now they make up 10 per cent of the workforce. Other initiatives include a Timpson university to embed skills into society, and support for chosen charities.

'If your business is just about making money it's hollow,' says James, 'and people are far more engaged with businesses which have social purpose rather than those that are just about making money.'

Could you get a better evocation of the Kindness Economy in action?

Tiny tweaks

Change, then, starts with you, and can be almost limitless in its ambition. This doesn't mean I am going to ask you to rip up your entire business strategy today and throw your organization off a metaphorical cliff. Nor am I going to ask you to boycott every business that doesn't yet have Timpson's values, or throw away – or, better, repurpose or recycle – every item in your house that isn't produced by a company with strong corporate social responsibility values. The first changes can be small. But it's that heartbeat that fuels one change to the next. That starts a movement.

I will be guiding you through the questions that you need to be asking yourself as you open yourself up to change. The questions build an understanding of what you need in this new economy; they guide you to figuring out your own Kindness Economy path. Small steps that lead you down your own unique path to change.

Harvard psychologist Susan David, in her book *Emotional Agility*, outlines what she calls 'the tiny tweaks principle' – the idea that small changes in behaviour feed back into more small changes and gradually accumulate. The very human truth is that if our approach is too grandiose, the possibility of failure becomes a burden in itself. But if we aim for tiny tweaks, we free ourselves to try. As she says, change is a process, not an event: 'Tweaking your mindset, motivation and habits is about turning your heart toward the fluidity of the world, rather than planting your feet on its stability.' This is about that journey of turning your heart.

Remember too that not everything has to be upended. People are still the same. Maslow's hierarchy of needs still holds good, and businesses are still in the game of servicing them. You will still be recognizable at the end of the process: you will just be the best, most responsible version you can be.

It's a bit like eating healthily. Tell yourself on a Monday that you're going to overhaul your entire diet, chuck out the calories and never eat junk again, and it's pretty much guaranteed that by Friday you'll be back on the pepperoni pizza. But make it a journey of discovery, where you change your thinking, start to learn, start to appreciate and seek out the good things that you yourself find delicious, and in a month's time you'll find your fridge is loaded with the greenest and freshest the grocer has to offer.

The skills to thrive

When I started writing about, thinking about and talking about the values that mattered to me in my last book, *Work Like a Woman*, it became more and more clear that a new set of business attributes were rising to the surface, like bubbles, throughout the business world. The more striking success stories were powered by the kinds of characteristics that traditional business models tended to think of as a bit 'soft'. I saw around me highly effective companies that were prioritizing creativity, humanity and true communication. That were thinking hard about the wellbeing of their employees. That were putting creative risk and ideas at the centre. That were using technological savvy to open themselves up to their customers in unprecedented ways. And that were breaking the boundaries of business progress while doing so. These were anything but soft in their outcomes.

They were instinctively giving themselves the edge by using a whole new set of skills – traditionally called the 'soft skills' that used to be relegated to the HR or marketing departments while the big boys of the boardroom sweated the numbers. The kind of skills that we tend to associate more with women. As I discovered in *Work Like a Woman*, businesses that succeed in this new landscape are more and more prioritizing what we think of as 'feminine' characteristics, in contrast to the tough-talking, hard-negotiating, masculine skill set that has been valued for so long. This is success powered by a female energy.

These soft skills are not soft skills at all. In fact, they are bloody hard to live up to. These are what we call thrive skills, and they are taking centre stage. They are the new powers you need, though they are as old as time. We have suppressed them in business – they got lost in the endless drilling for data and analytics and statistical breakdowns and all those dry words that signify we are looking in the rear-view mirror to set our course.

Women, I believe, will be key to this shift. First, because we largely drive purchasing decisions and thus hold huge economic power in our hands. We've been distanced from this for aeons now: the caring work we do is largely unpaid and unrecognized, the jobs we gravitate towards are lower-paid than those dominated by men. Consistent economic devaluation has made us lose sight of our immense financial clout. By driving the consumer spending that we mostly control responsibly, we can create huge waves of change.

And then there's the fact that empathy for ourselves and others is at the heart of the Kindness Economy – and it's something women often excel at.

Ignore these skills at your peril. As many formerly revered processes like diagnosing diseases and delivering justice become mechanized, power in the future is going to be determined by how effectively you draw on the deep wells of these soft skills. Business advantage will lie with organizations who have compassion and empathy at their core.

As an illustration, look at the countries that have most effectively steered their way through the Covid-19 pandemic. New Zealand. Finland. Denmark. Taiwan. Norway. What do they have in common? They are led by women. The countries at the other end of the scale? The US, Brazil, the UK. All countries led at the outset of the pandemic by 'strong man' leaders, good at the bombast and priding themselves on their tough deal-making and their ability to 'win' at all costs.

This isn't a statistical anomaly, or a coincidence. It is that progressive governments led by women (surrounded in most cases by men who equally understand the value of these soft skills) were already adept at using the exact qualities that turned out to be crucial to navigating this disaster: Openness. Humanity. Intuition. Courage. Agility. Honesty. Listening. Communication. Empathy. A willingness to act quickly, to make hard decisions by drawing on a deep-seated compassion.

The countries that got in most trouble were the ones where the governments were characterized by politicking, manipulating, blame-shifting and obfuscation. Great ways to elbow your way to the top. Less use when you have to make impossible life-or-death calls in an unprecedented situation.

Because make no mistake, the skills we are talking about might be called 'soft', but in practice they are tough as hell. We have already met Jacqueline Novogratz, a woman who really inspires me. The CEO of global non-profit venture capital firm Acumen, whose goal is to tackle global poverty by entrepreneurial means, she is used to operating in the most challenging of business terrains, for the highest of stakes. In a podcast with journalist Krista Tippett, she said something that caught my attention: '[These are] not actually the soft skills. When I was growing up, we relegated skills like the moral imagination, like listening, like understanding identity, as a tool rather than as a bludgeon, holding opposites without rejecting either side – those are the hard skills.'

When I wrote *Work Like a Woman*, I identified some of these 'soft skills' that are so necessary today, and as I teased out the Kindness Economy principles that we looked at in the last chapter, I realized that what you need to implement them starts with those very same tools:

• Courage, rather than bravery. Bravery is a rushing-in. Courage is facing up to the hard stuff. Think of the courage involved in locking down your country at the first sign of trouble, as Jacinda Ardern did.

• Vision, rather than ambition. Ambition is centred on the self. But, as we know, the Kindness Economy demands a wider horizon.

• Perseverance, rather than dominance. The Kindness Economy is a shared enterprise, a collaboration. The desire to conquer and dominate is not going to cut it here.

• Emotional openness. You need to be able to listen to and communicate the deeper truths, not just the brand 'messaging'. In the new landscape, customers respond to and demand honesty.

• Wisdom, rather than knowledge. In an internet age, knowledge is easily acquired or faked. Wisdom is hard-learned.

• Resilience, rather than ironclad 'invulnerability'. The bough that bends in the wind is going to last through more storms than the rigid pole. There will be setbacks; how will you weather them?

• Collaboration, rather than splendid isolation. Hone the instinct that draws inspiration from as wide a frame as possible.

- Determination, rather than single-mindedness. By all means set your course for the North Star of your business. But remember to lift your eyes to the view around you as you go – it will help guide you there by the best route.

I'd like to add another skill: creative instinct. Now, there's a whole chapter on this later. But I mention it here because it's a core human skill that I believe has never been more important in this increasingly left-brain, data-driven world of ours. I'm not talking creative genius here (part of the reason we don't see creativity in more places is this ridiculous reverence it carries). I'm talking about that *feeling* that comes from your gut and makes the back of your eyes fizz – and which probably solves a problem, or some sort of tension, that no machine could ever get to.

It's all about evolution and, as Darwin argued, our capacity as humans for ethics – our refined moral sense, our conscience – is a powerful survival mechanism. It is one of the things that give our species the edge in the struggle for existence. This works for business too: as a whole, we will survive and progress if we evolve to build an increased conscience into what we do.

Ultimately, forging a thriving business is not about switching off your desire for commerce, or your desire to build, or to make or to sell or to buy. It's about looking at whatever it is that you do and thinking, 'How can I nurture this business in a way that also nurtures the world?'

You might find the word 'nurturing' rather odd when we're talking about how businesses can do better, but I am using this language deliberately. Look where 'Be the best and sod the rest' has got us.

What we need now are the words that we use when we are really at our best. When we are in love. When we parent. This new way of doing business is about embedding our human skills more deeply into business practice and into the way we all buy, sell, work and live.

I've lost count over the years of the number of people I've come across in business who are ruthless, lacking in compassion, focused on individual wins over the collective good. Meet them in their domestic, off-duty lives and they're often working for a local charity, active in their communities and massive fans of *Bake Off*.

Why? Why is there this division between the selves we show in our private existences, and the ones we display in our business lives? If we can bring these two sides of ourselves into the workplace, then that is the first step in building businesses based on human values that thrive.

The very word 'kindness' in the Kindness Economy is carefully chosen: this isn't just about ethics, or abstract morality. This is about a considerate, generous, respectful, humane way of behaving. Kindness isn't soft. It is powerful.

Purpose done proper

So we've dug deep, put empathy to work, embraced new skills that have the power to transform a company culture. We now need to rally behind a common goal. A North Star. And I don't mean 'grow more than last year' or 'beat brand X'. I mean figuring out *why* a business exists, what it adds to make the world better. What we have now all come to understand as 'purpose'.

Now, purpose done well is fundamental. By done well I mean driving a business's entire ethos, its behaviours, its communications – its every interaction with people – from the inside out. Far from a CSR initiative shoved in some corner of a business calendar, it should connect what a business sells with what it believes will make lives better. And indeed investors, as well as the markets, now demand this. In 2020, there was a notable increase in analysis and requests for information on environmental and social issues from investors. According to financial research at Refinitiv Lipper, a total of €290 billion, constituting over half of fund flows in Europe, went into ESG (environmental, social and governance) products. Look what happens when you fall foul of this: doubts about the way Deliveroo treats its workers led to investors getting cold feet about their IPO, with several of the largest announcing that they would not invest in the company.

As consumers, we are increasingly used to businesses brandishing their purposes at us. But I believe that we are also increasingly wised up to the ones that are little more than slogans.

Here's a story about 'purpose' done, well, shit.

In the months after my book *Work Like a Woman* was published in 2018, the Portas team and I were called by many businesses who wanted to look at how they could make their culture, practices and products work better for women. Many of the meetings followed a similar pattern but I'm going to home in on one with a well-known British brand. The conversation went like this.

'We're so pleased to meet you,' I said, sitting beside my CEO Caireen and other female members of the Portas team. 'How would you like us to help you?'

Around the table were mostly white men, all wearing grey suits, and a couple of women in grey suits too.

'We know our product is bought mostly by women but

the way we sell it is ironically geared more towards men,' said one of the grey suits. 'We want to work with you on a "brand purpose" campaign that shows female consumers we get them and serve them better than any other brand.'

'Why the change?' I asked. 'You've done well so far with how you've done things. What is it that you really want to achieve?'

'We want to broaden our market.'

'I understand that. And it's clear what your financial goals are. But what are the other reasons why you want to do that?'

Cue a frame from a David Attenborough documentary, the one in which all the lemmings hear a noise and their necks extend upwards en masse, with heads at a slight tilt and eyes fixed fearfully on the horizon. The grey suits all did that. They stared at me uncomprehendingly. What on earth did I mean? What other point could there possibly be than selling more units?

It was one of many meetings we walked away from knowing that we wouldn't be able to work well with the organization. Driven by a 'purpose' someone had written on a slide, they had no sense of what that purpose actually meant. More worryingly – they just didn't care.

Purpose has enjoyed a meteoric rise in marketing circles, most famously on the back of Simon Sinek's eminently sensible *Find Your Why*.

At Portas, we embrace *purpose* – but we find it more helpful to think of it as your *philosophy*. Not to be contrary (although I'm rather happy to be accused of not conforming) but because it forces the 'how' – *how* a business lives, breathes and acts on what it believes, in the real world.

Philosophy has a beautiful meaning in the dictionary: 'an activity people undertake when they seek to understand fundamental truths about themselves, the world in which they live, and their relationships to the world and to each other'. In the last chapter we looked at role models. Again, it starts with us as individuals: a deep understanding of what we believe and how we connect with others. Our philosophies as individuals are not separate from our business philosophies: they need to be one and the same.

In our businesses, a philosophy can't be confined to a slide. Or a one-off marketing stunt. It is unique to you and your business. A social compass, guiding your way. And once you have it, it ignites humanity in everything you do. 'This is how I am. This is how I am being with people.' My team and I call this the 'people experience' or PX of a business. It goes deeper than customer experience because it puts people first.

And that's what it's all about: an understanding of ourselves, the world around us and the relationships that bind us all together. That is the Kindness Economy in action. Put simply, the Kindness Economy rests on folding the basic human values of decency and compassion into business practices. And I believe that's about creating a business culture that is more human than it has been for a long time.

A final thought: for the last years while I've been on the road with this Kindness Economy theory, giving talks and doing podcasts, writing newsletters, I often get a certain type of feedback. I'll talk about the great strides a particular company is making – how they are placing sustainability at their core, or focusing on employee wellbeing. How they have quietly revolutionized their supply chain, or developed a fantastic community initiative. But there will always be a dissenting voice, saying: 'I've heard they aren't up to speed with their accreditations' or 'They're still not at carbon negative.'

We need to stop doing this. As I said in Chapter 3, this is a process of change and, as yet, nobody is at 100 per cent in every area. Nobody has all the answers, including me. If we pull everyone up every time they fall short of perfect, we hamstring all attempts at progress. The more we celebrate the journey to understanding, the faster we will travel it. Some of the organizations that are doing this best understand that walking the walk is always going to involve the odd stumble.

Progress comes when we acknowledge our shortcomings and try to overcome them. This, for instance, comes from the fashion brand Ganni's responsibility statement, under the heading 'The Elephant in the Room': 'As a fashion brand we're the first to admit we're behind. In the past we haven't shouted about our efforts because we're scared of being called out for greenwashing. Fashion is problematic, and driven by newness . . .' What follows is a list of the things they think they should be doing better at, in among the large suite of forty-four forward-thinking and impressive initiatives they have already implemented, that cover a range of issues from people to production. In actuality, they are a company willing to ask the difficult questions.

That is where change starts.

TO DO
Put your philosophy to work

Does your brand have a purpose? Whether you call it a mission statement, a North Star, or a philosophy (as we do), I'm willing to bet it does.

If so, where in your organization can you see it? Is it threaded through everything that you do? Are you living and breathing it daily? Is it informing all your ideas and your strategies? Does everybody in your organization understand what it is, and why?

Or is it mostly visible on your website, in your advertising, and popping up as jazzy slogans at conferences?

Simon Sinek rightly and famously posited three questions to ask in figuring out your organization's purpose: *why?*, *how?* and *what?*

A great starting point. But what I have noticed over the years is that businesses spend a lot of time answering the *why?* and the *what?* but neglect to look at the *how?* How is that purpose showing up in your company? How is it guiding your strategy? How is it informing your practices? Because if all it is doing is decorating your labelling, then you need to ask yourself some questions:

● *Is it the right purpose?* Too often organizations brainstorm themselves into statements that are too lofty. High-minded and ambitious, they lack the connection to what the brand actually does. Which leads to a fizzy drinks company running an ad where a supermodel brings peace to a protest.

- *Do I believe it?* Not 'Do I believe this is a good way to think?', but 'Do I truly believe in what we are doing?'

- If you're convinced it *is* the right purpose, then *why isn't it working harder for us?* This is where you have to ask the tough questions: have I communicated it to my people properly, do they understand and feel excited by it? Is it being lived, truly, across every part of the business and customer experience – or does it only ever make an appearance in forgotten slides and a couple of ad campaigns? Is it driving my future innovation, as well as shaping the here and now? If there is a small but loud group of people who aren't on board and are generating cynicism – are they the right people to have in the business . . . ?

Let's make sure our purpose, our philosophy, can truly catch fire.

6

Who's in Your Web?

In 1624, the poet John Donne eloquently expressed the essential interconnection that links the whole of humanity. 'No man is an island, entire of itself,' he wrote. 'Every man is a piece of the continent, a part of the main.'

It's a timeless truth. But while previous generations were acutely aware of it, we became increasingly distanced from it in the age of individualism. Then came Covid. The pandemic showed us just how interconnected we all are as we each powerfully confronted our individual responsibility for the wellbeing of the whole – and how much the wellbeing of the whole benefits us individually. We started to see the invisible threads running between us all, people and planet. We started to feel that by raising you up, so I am raised. We were forced to reconnect with this truth. Even the very breath we exhaled could potentially impact another's life. 'Me' and 'we' became inextricably bound as awareness of the hive mind and consequent behaviours became more powerful than ever.

Four hundred years after Donne – and almost a year into Covid – president and CEO of the international healthcare organization Project Hope, Rabih Torbay, echoed Donne's thought as he considered the impact of the pandemic. He wrote of how the virus has given us evidence of how interconnected the world is in how it has spread worldwide. But, as he points out, it is that very interconnectedness, and the sense of empathy it can bring with it, that will lie at the core of how we take our next steps.

Indeed it will. We cannot better rebuild our future if we don't honour this renewed awareness of our interconnection – and allow it to influence every decision we make.

The ripple effect

In business, every decision we make is meaningful, not just within an organization but beyond. The ripples spread. We are one gigantic living organism and must embrace the impact of our business that reverberates beyond our own boundaries.

Unlike many areas of business in which decisions can be made without being confronted forcefully by the knock-on effects, interconnection has underpinned my whole career because it's inescapable in retail. It was what I was trying to address with my High Street Report in 2011. Shops closing on a high street does not just signify heartbreak for the business owners; it can kick off a vicious circle where the neighbourhood declines, the properties become devalued, and the remaining shops are endangered. And those are just the local effects – retail typically relies on goods manufactured halfway round the world, using practices, good or bad, which have far-reaching impact. To say nothing of the environmental ramifications.

Let me give you a living and breathing example of the positive power of interconnection in action.

Thinking about the trio of chicken shops, betting shops and charity shops that signify a declining area, my team and I at Portas thought: what if we took one of those and proved the power of retail to act as a heartbeat on every high street?

So, we chose charity shops. (I wasn't going to touch the betting shops and I don't know how to fry chicken.)

We wanted to provide a chain of charity shops called Mary's Living & Giving. Shops that not only gave joy to communities, but also could have a deep effect on them.

After taking the concept to various charities, Save the Children – headed by Tanya Steele and Jayne Cartwright – came on board. (Do I need to say that it wasn't a coincidence that the people who 'got' what we were trying to do happened to be women?)

With every shop, we edit the stock, redecorate the store and replace racks stuffed with Aunt Enid's old knickerbockers with the best product beautifully displayed. This then creates the crucial next step: drawn by how inviting the shop looks, people donate really good stuff. They feel good sending their clothes somewhere they know will showcase them brilliantly and get a decent price – this in turn benefits someone in need of Save the Children. That's the core of the whole thing: the shop and the charity.

But then you get into the amazing butterfly effect that is so apparent in great retail. Whenever we opened a new shop, we found that local people with expertise in interior design, arts or anything creative gave their time for free, to create murals perhaps, or graphics, because they knew their work would be shown in a great setting – and benefit a good cause. They felt good giving back to their community.

Then there were those who wanted to work in the shops: from people who were looking for experience in retail but hadn't previously thought of working in a charity shop, to those who had been out of work for a while and wanted to get back into the rhythm or freelancers between jobs.

And then, of course, there are the people coming in to buy.

Quite quickly, Mary's Living & Giving became a magnet. Customers flocked to the shops, knowing they are fantastic spaces with amazing stock. Councils wanted them on their high street, because footfall goes up – and if someone pops into Mary's Living & Giving, they'll invariably drop into another shop on the same street.

Today we have twenty-six shops that have generated more than £30 million in income. I really am proud of this work. It means a lot to me. The root, of course, is the people in need who are helped by Save the Children. But the branches of this tree, the far wider effect, like that created by a butterfly flapping its wings in the jungle and setting off a chain of events that culminates in good for everybody, is the interconnection of the whole experience. These shops benefit not only the people who work in them and those who buy, but also the place where they are located – and, of course, the planet, because of all the product that is reused and reloved.

Recently, Mary's Living & Giving partnered with the designers Teatum Jones and Liberty for a Zero Waste collection. Teatum Jones as designers are already living and breathing the Kindness Economy philosophy, using local communities as inspiration, finding innovative ways to reuse and repurpose materials, and this new sustainable partnership is another beautiful tendril of interconnectedness stemming from the Living & Giving idea.

It's one proof that we are all part of a vast web and, just as the fly tugging on the side alerts the spider hiding in the centre, each of us has the power to create impact. And it's the reason why the Kindness Economy is so important – we aren't just tidying up our own little area of operations, we are making a chain of consequences. But we can't do it alone. Interconnectedness is like one of those magic eye pictures:

once you have seen it you can't unsee it. It becomes the back-drop to every decision you make.

Everything is transparent

Savvy companies are putting interconnection at the top of their agendas, for the simple reason that the market is beginning to demand it. Businesses are now more than ever exposed to public scrutiny, with the walls of organizations turning to glass, as trend company TrendWatching points out in a 2017 report. Where once brands worked in splendid, opaque isolation, the ways you conduct your business are now more transparent than ever. Your processes, your alliances, your ethics – all of them are up for inspection, and the 'I couldn't have known' defence doesn't wash any more. As TrendWatching puts it: 'in an age of radical transparency, your internal culture is your brand'.

Every time we see a company burying their heads or shirking their responsibilities, public faith gets that little bit more eroded. Public faith that is already paper-thin in some sectors: think of the 2008 financial crash and the impunity with which the banking sector seemed to be playing fast and loose with financial instruments that would affect all our lives. Think of Volkswagen, riding roughshod over regulations that are there to preserve the very planet we live on. Think of the broken ladder of corporate responsibility and accountability that led to the horrors of the Grenfell fire. Nobody watching the Grenfell Inquiry unfold could not lament the cascade of decisions – cost-cutting, buck-passing, bureaucracy and corporate obfuscation – that resulted in that cladding being put on the building.

For an example of a business turning a blind eye to the

effects of interconnectedness, take Boohoo. In June 2020 serious questions arose over exploitative working conditions in some of their suppliers and their subcontractors in Leicester. It appeared that unsafe sweatshops paying considerably less than the minimum wage were part of the supply chain to the giant internet retailer (which, meanwhile, was coining it in due to its online advantage during the lockdowns).

Boohoo immediately commissioned an independent review, which came to the conclusion that, although the company had not directly exploited workers or broken the law, it had ignored red flags in its supply chain. Boohoo's response was to give their suppliers and subcontractors a deadline to bring all their manufacturing in-house and, as of March 2021, they have cut ties with hundreds of previous suppliers who did not meet the required standards.

Good news that unsafe sweatshops that are exploiting their workers are no longer being propped up by our desire for the latest trend perhaps (though I gather that these places tend to pop up again as soon as they are shut down). But this solution seems to be just pushing responsibility down the chain. Beyond the results of the independent review which were critical of the company, and the accompanying media scrutiny, there is no accountability for a business model which sells garments for pennies and which has in the past relied on easily exploited labour.

This is what can happen when interconnectedness gets ignored, when corporate cultures lose the basic thread of human empathy.

Because in the end that is what interconnectedness comes down to: empathy. Not a wishy-washy 'I feel your pain' kind of empathy, but a rational, kind, fundamental and sincere ability to put yourself in another's place. Real empathy is a compassionate understanding that how we treat people matters, that it makes logical sense to think of the universal as well as the individual, and that working for our own gain at others' expense is a route to disaster.

In our globalized, international economy, each of us holds threads that connect us to each other. These threads – a giant gossamer web – link us all with a common humanity. We should celebrate this interconnectedness as a lifeline, because it also means we hold the means to improve the wider picture. Moving forward, we must drive a collective shift in our approach to decision-making that puts interconnectedness – and the consequences of our actions – at the centre of what we do.

It will be a powerful shift that will move us from the two-dimensional tunnel lens of so much current thinking towards a far more multi-faceted view of our collective landscape.

Twist your thinking

In business, interconnectedness means we can't make decisions in splendid isolation, thinking only of the effect on our own bottom lines. It also means we can't make them behind closed doors. Instead, we need to twist our thinking and look at the potential benefits that interconnectedness brings. Your core purposes can cascade out and become so much more. Large businesses clearly have the potential to create greatest impact. But think of the decisions you make in a smaller business as part of a much larger whole – that has huge capacity to create change too.

Covid has shown us many examples of how our business decisions can impact – the good and the bad.

During the first lockdown in March 2020, for instance, a

remarkable alliance sprang up between giant multinationals McDonald's and Aldi in Germany. With fast-food outlets closed, and the need for supermarket workers rising, McDonald's offered its employees the opportunity to work for Aldi for the duration. Aldi would be able to cope with the surge in demand for its services, McDonald's would retain more of its staff, and the employees themselves had the chance of staying in employment. The simple question – 'Could our employees be useful elsewhere in these extraordinary times?' – became an initiative that had knock-on beneficial effects, not just for the two companies involved, but for their employees, the communities they served, and ultimately for taxpayers.

On the flip side, the powers that be at MGM announced they would be delaying the release of their juggernaut James Bond film for the second time in October 2020. On one level, with countries around the world swinging in and out of lockdowns, this was logical in financial terms: they were trying to protect their cashflow. But the ramifications across the industry were huge: for cinemas desperately trying to stay on their feet it was a hammer blow. Cineworld alone immediately shuttered almost 700 cinemas across the UK and the US, placing 45,000 jobs into a precarious state. Now it might not be fair to lay this entirely at the feet of MGM, given the obvious difficulties that cinema-going posed during a pandemic. Nevertheless, it was a decision with ramifications for the whole industry. Bond's worldwide audience, hungry for the moment of lightness in dark times, was disappointed. If the studios want to get us back in there, marvelling in the dark at the silver screen, we need to know they will continue to provide the magic even when times are tough.

Couldn't MGM have found a third way, one that protected their product, but recognized how many different companies and jobs relied on them? Delay the new film, yes. But surely it would have been possible to relicense older ones for a short period to allow cinemas to get valuable customers through the doors in anticipation of the new film?

In spite of the 'we're all in this together' rhetoric, during lockdown too many businesses acted to protect themselves first at whatever cost. Faced with the unavoidable reality that they were going to take a hit, they turned round and tried to pass the pain on, cancelling orders, cutting down on work for others and slashing the amount they were willing to pay to those they usually rely on.

I get it. When the going gets tough, it's tempting for those at the top of the food chain to shield themselves. That's just 'business', you might argue. But this approach leaves each of us vulnerable. Every business relies on a complex web of supply chains, outside agencies, contractors and outlets. As businesses we pay these people because we need them and their work is valuable to us: is it reasonable then to cut them off when times get hard?

'We must look at any given situation or problem from the front and from the back, from the sides, and from the top and the bottom, so from at least six different angles,' says the Dalai Lama in *The Book of Joy*. 'This allows us to take a more complete and holistic view of reality, and if we do, our response will be more constructive.'

Much as I'd like to improve on his wisdom, I think I'll leave you with that thought.

TO DO

Draw your web

As businesses, our interconnections are legion and complex.

Remember the spider diagrams you had to draw at school when creating and planning? It's time for one of those.

Put yourself in the middle, and then move outwards to draw the first circle. This will be your internal connections: your employees; your investors; your direct stakeholders.

Next, the most direct of your external connections: your clients; your suppliers; your collaborators; your mentors.

In the next ring, put the communities you form part of: physical – your local community; virtual – your online community; your sector; your professional associations; your competitors.

Outside of that, the interconnections formed by your impact on the wider world; the environmental effects of your products; your subcontractors.

Now is the time to interrogate the model you have drawn further. Dig deep: have you left anybody out? Talk to people within the organizations you have listed. Can they add rings to your diagram? It's astonishing what you will learn.

When you are satisfied that your diagram is as full as you can make it, look at the quality of all the connections. Are they as strong as they should be? Are you putting the energy and resources of your organization into the right places?

How does your company strategy affect all these connections? How will your future strategic decisions impact them?

To flip it around to the other perspective, when you are buying, is the company you are buying from giving you a sense that it is considering its impact in all these areas? As consumers we cannot be expected to audit every company we interact with. Nonetheless, if a trusted brand is clearly indicating that it considers its interconnections, that's a good reason to buy from it.

Done properly, this map of your interconnections is a valuable tool in auditing the impact your organization has in the world. But, more than that, it is a tool that can help you pinpoint your position in the world, and look at your business with fresh eyes.

7

What's Your Double V?

I didn't come from a middle-class background. My parents were Irish immigrants who arrived in Watford in the late fifties and soon had a family of five children to raise. My dad worked in sales and my mother knew the importance of budgeting. Trotting along behind her to all the local shops, I absorbed from her the concept of good value.

Somehow, though, over the years, the meaning of 'good value' has changed. 'Value' has become synonymous with 'cheap' or, to use marketing-speak, 'affordable'. It sounds noble: why should people be denied choice and variety and fun stuff just because they aren't wealthy?

But let's pick it apart a bit, because what seems to be missing from this interpretation of 'value' is the word that for my mother's generation automatically preceded it: *good* value. This isn't the same as cheap, which does nothing for society, nothing for the planet, and nothing for people's wellbeing.

So, when Channel 4 approached me in 2012 to make a series on UK manufacturing, I initially refused. They wanted to see if we could make a £5 pair of jeans to compete with Primark while using UK manufacturing. I never wanted to do that show. It would have been a race to the bottom.

My question was, 'Can't we turn this on its head? Can't we make a product that captures the true value of UK manufacturing instead?' My team and I went back to Channel 4 and said: no, we'll do it if we can create our own brand. We wanted to make a product that was slightly more expensive but that we believed would give *real* good value: not only in its price, and its quality, but in what its production could do for society. We came up with the product: Kinky Knickers – a brand of mid-market underwear, proudly made in Britain.

Instead of denim, we wanted to ask the question: would people be prepared to pay a little more for something made in this country? What if they knew that it was providing employment and apprenticeships, contributing to long-term skills? It wouldn't be a show-off purchase – this is underwear, it's out of sight – but it would be lace, handmade here. (M&S, the biggest supplier of the nation's knickers, had been the last to go offshore with their manufacturing.) Would we be able to compete? I wanted to see whether it is practically possible – and financially viable – to restart production here in Britain again.

Our goal wasn't just about putting people in employment, but starting apprenticeships that can stoke long-term skills. If we could get people to buy into the idea of the brand, rather than just buying nice pants, we could start a ball rolling that might just be transformative. There was a lot to do. We had to find a factory that could help us and track down the right machinery for production because so much of it has been sent abroad. But then we reached the real sticking point: machinists. We needed to be able to train up a new generation.

Back in the day, Middleton used to be one of the biggest manufacturing districts in Manchester and these factories didn't just produce textiles – they fed a community. Mothers worked alongside their daughters. Families passed the skills from generation to generation. Local shops and cafes served the factory workers with their morning teas and their lunch-time sandwiches; income provided from the workers' wages kept the neighbourhood economy afloat. It was a whole community with a sense of common purpose. It was a thriving ecosystem.

But then the race to the bottom to create the cheapest possible fashions at the highest possible profit started. Production moved abroad and the factories closed down. Many of the brands themselves are still in our shops – churning out more and more items of fast-fashion clothing that will eventually end up in landfill. But the factories that fed them have gone, the jobs too – and with them all the shoots and tendrils that make up a thriving community.

We got the factory going again, working with scores of people – many of whom had never been employed before – who queued up when we advertised our new jobs. Some came from families in which nobody had had steady employment for years. So much of what these young adults should have inherited had been hollowed out. They'd lost their sense of self and the whole social infrastructure that used to bind the neighbourhood.

But bit by bit, together with some brilliant people, we started to turn a small piece of that around. We created a fantastic knicker brand, but, more than that, a sense of self and of purpose. We played a tiny part in reanimating the heartbeat at the centre of that community. Kinky Knickers is still going to this day.

I've told this story before, forgive me. But I love it. It's the story I think about whenever I hear the argument that mass-market brands – in clothing, in food, in housewares, in anything – are there to 'democratize' by driving their prices ever lower and piling their stuff ever higher. What is the point of cheaper 'value' goods, if the real cost of them is jobs, livelihoods, entire communities?

Do we need 'democratization'?

Twenty years ago, discussions with brands about what businesses could do for society usually focused on one thing: how to make things affordable and accessible to as many people as possible.

There was some worth to this argument, and some innovative disruptors who brought surprisingly good quality along with low prices. But too quickly it became a race to the bottom – rails and shelves laden with cheap goods destined to be thrown out after a couple of uses. Environmentally wasteful practices and low-cost labour: a constant drive to keep the churn going.

Businesses told us, 'We're bringing you cheap stuff: this is value, it's making your life better.' What they didn't tell us was what they were taking away from us in the process of giving. The example of Middleton is just one of many such stories about what we lost, in the quest for cheapness.

In the UK more than £30 billion worth of clothing sits at the back of wardrobes. That £140 million worth of clothing in landfill that I referred to earlier? That's 350,000 tonnes a year. We know that the industry puts pressure on our water resources and pollutes the environment, with global textile production releasing 1.2 billion tonnes of greenhouse gases into the atmosphere annually.

And we keep buying more each year. Because we can. Because it's cheap.

If all this costs us our wellbeing and our planet then it's too expensive. Fact.

We are in a time of economic crisis. Financial uncertainty has become the only sure thing on the horizon – the unknowns are legion. Which means there is a tendency among businesses and retail to generate income by going ever lower on price. Isn't that what the potentially cash-strapped customer is going to want? Rock-bottom price tags and as many special offers as you can throw at them?

Take the grocery sector. At a time when a shameful number of people are relying on food banks in the UK, perhaps supermarkets *should* be doing everything that they can right now to get food on to people's plates as cheaply as possible and hang the consequences. Unfortunately, though, 'make everything cheaper' is not a viable solution. It's a short-term fix that creates a longer-term problem. The idea that low prices are just there to 'democratize' goods, as though the whole economic system is a charitable enterprise, is faulty. It leads to waste.

Cheap food is a myth. In a 2017 report, the Sustainable Food Trust estimated that for every £1 spent on food by British consumers, an extra £1 of hidden costs was incurred – and it's passed right back on to us. Of every one of those hidden pounds, 37.3p is incurred by the costs of diet-related disease. Over 35p is incurred by natural capital degradation together with biodiversity loss. We're paying a very heavy price indeed for all those disposable BOGOF deals.

So how cheap is cheap food, really? In fact, can we as a society afford it?

I don't have the solutions to this problem. I wish I did. But I do know that if people are short of money, the answer is not feeding them cheaply produced crap that damages their health and the world we live in.

The price of principles

It is possible to combine progressive values with a fair price. In late 2019 I visited New York, and was taken aback by the strange feel of the city. Where once it had hummed with energy, it felt curiously lifeless: the 'greed is good, more is more' culture that used to power the place seemed to have stalled. Most of the shops felt flat: grand, stylish and painstakingly curated, but somehow dead.

There was one exception, though – one shop we visited that felt truly teeming and vibrant: the Patagonia store. Patagonia was packed. That is a business founded on the values of its creator – Yvon Chouinard. It grew out of his passion for climbing, and his determination (unusual at the time) to leave the mountains he climbed as pristine as he found them. Patagonia isn't rock bottom in terms of prices, but neither is it high end. It makes room in its prices for its principles, and asks that we consider our purchases carefully.

The sight of that shop set me to thinking about Black Friday – my least favourite shopping day of the year, when retailers become a frenzy of red stickers and a carnival of consumption for its own sake.

On Black Friday 2011 Patagonia ran a striking ad featuring one of their classic fleeces with the headline: 'Don't Buy This Jacket.' On the most iconic day for peak consumerism, the message from this brand was counterintuitive: stop buying, and think.

The body of the text under the headline celebrated the Common Threads Initiative, Patagonia's pledge to their customers to repair their clothing for as long as the customer needs it, and to help the customer sell on the jacket if it is no longer needed. It's a simple idea, but as an ad it was revolutionary: buy this item only if you need it, consider its impact, pass it on when you can, and keep it out of landfill.

It wasn't a gimmick: this is what the brand believes. Every year, they use Black Friday to push an alternative message. In 2016, they donated all their revenue for the day to environmental causes. Not their profits – their revenue. They gave away about $10 million. But what they gained was huge: a brand that people implicitly trust. And the fruits of this were clearly visible on my visit to New York.

Patagonia is extremely successful by any measure – in 2018 it was worth $1 billion. But for its founder, profit is not the overriding issue. Here is Yvon Chouinard: 'At the end of the year, we measure success by how much good we've done and what impact we're having on society, not by profit. Honestly, if you ask me how much money we've made in the last year, I would have to look it up. I know that we are extremely profitable.'

The Patagonia story is a celebration of what a brand can do if it decouples itself from the whirling frenzy of consumerism. It is a business that has scaled huge heights, a business that instinctively operates by all the values of the Kindness Economy. What it doesn't do is put a premium on price and profit margin.

So let's think about Black Friday – who does it work for? Who wins from it?

Well, Black Friday generates massive revenue for the retail sector – £8.6 billion in the UK in 2019. Perhaps we should be feeding this hideous beast?

No. Every pound spent is a vote and Black Friday is a landslide for cheapness. No other values are in the frame. It's a frenzy of consumption for its own sake. And it reached its nadir in 2020 with PrettyLittleThing's little black dress which went on sale for 8p. This generated deservedly outraged headlines about unsustainable consumption. We cannot keep kidding ourselves that somewhere in the world there isn't someone paying a much higher price for our right to buy a whole outfit for pennies, wear it once and then chuck it away.

But there are some hopeful voices singing out a different song, using the annual feeding frenzy to push a more interesting agenda. Here are a couple more examples that gladdened my heart recently:

Everlane: alleviating hunger
Since 2013, Everlane, an ethical clothing company based in the US, has raised money annually for their Black Friday Fund, which tackles a different cause every year. In 2020, with hunger looming for many Americans, they partnered with Feeding America to try to provide 2 million meals for people in need. They started by donating $100,000, which they then raised in line with customer donations. In the end they smashed their target, raising enough to fund over 2 million meals.

Allbirds: tackling climate change
The New Zealand footwear company Allbirds actually raised their prices on Black Friday, donating the extra dollar, plus one more from their own coffers, to Greta Thunberg's Fridays for Future movement.

Freitag: exchanging products
Meanwhile, Swiss bag company Freitag shut its online store entirely on Black Friday, instead sending its site visitors to its

SWAP (Shopping Without Any Payment) site, where they could exchange pre-used bags with other customers and break the new purchase cycle for the day.

OVO energy: exploring nature
And OVO energy, a Bristol-based ethical energy provider, went with a promotion to help people go green on Black Friday. Instead of a discount incentive they gave a £50 National Trust gift card for signing up on that day, in order to help people connect with nature.

These brands are interrupting the accelerated spiral of Black Friday splurges and asking us to recalibrate our thinking. They are asking the customer to consider different values that reflect a more thoughtful and exciting agenda.

So, while Black Friday maintains its stranglehold, you can use it to tune in to the 61 per cent of shoppers who believe that consumerism around large shopping events has got out of hand. Some 45 per cent of UK consumers said that sustainability was important in their shopping decisions, rising to 55 per cent among Gen Z and millennials. This is only going to increase.

As a business, you still need to offer your customers a proposition, but that proposition does not have to compete on price alone. Socially progressive values are a compelling reason for customers to buy from you, and they are becoming ever more so.

The brands who are challenging Black Friday give me hope. It's a wonderfully creative bubbling up of imagination, thought and care for people and planet, which brings uniqueness and vibrancy – and selling power – to their businesses. You won't win customers by delivering dry sermons but by singing joyfully about this new modern way of being. This is exciting, attractive stuff.

Oscar Wilde famously defined a cynic as 'A man who knows the price of everything, and the value of nothing.'

Let's not be cynics: let's not shackle ourselves to knowing only the price of things. Let's celebrate the things we care about: that is where real value lies.

TO DO
The Double V equation

Think of your perceived brand value. You can express it as an equation: value equals functional and emotional benefits divided by cost, or:

$$\text{Value} = \frac{\text{Functional and Emotional Benefits}}{\text{Cost}}$$

All I ask you to do is to bring another figure into the frame: values. Plural. So, the new value proposition is:

$$\text{Double V} = \frac{\text{Functional and Emotional Benefits} + \textbf{Values}}{\text{Cost}}$$

What your values are is particular to you, and should be as specific as possible. Are you rolling out plus-size ranges in your clothing? Are you committing to carbon negativity? Are you building longevity into your products? Can you aim to bring more values into the equation?

Is your Double V additive? Does it make a positive contribution?

8

Who's in Your Community?

As the weeks unwound over the various lockdowns of 2020, I found that the pattern of my days began to mirror the way my mother used to live. I would take my daily walk, making a visit to the greengrocer one day, the post office and newsagent's on another, the local Sainsbury's on the third.

Settling into my new routine, I was delighted to see the familiar faces (or should that be the familiar top halves of faces?) behind the tills and it became ever more clear to me that this network of shops was giving me so much more than the goods I was paying for.

I'd chat with Hong in the greengrocer's about how her home deliveries were doing, or find out from Zam in the post office about what was going on in the community centre where people were donating to food banks. I'd bump into neighbours and people from the area who I hadn't socialized with in months, happy to have a few minutes of conversation at a safe distance.

These moments of connection were nuggets of comfort in a sea of uncertainty – a sense that outside the four walls of my home, and the screen which had become the lifeline of my business, life was continuing.

High streets, marketplaces, town centres have been part of the way we live and breathe for millennia. They are places where we thrive and connect. They tap into fundamental needs because we're wired as humans for social interaction.

Imagine if we all ended up just clicking on our internet baskets from our own homes. How grey would the world be? The infrastructure of local businesses feeds our needs on a daily basis. They are crucial to the complex web of human connections. The countless tiny interactions that happen when we do something as simple as walk down the road to buy a pint of milk. These things are important.

The great urban planner and writer, Jane Jacobs, described it like this, in her book *The Death and Life of Great American Cities*: 'The trust of a city street is formed over time from many, many little public sidewalk contacts ... Most of it is ostensibly trivial, but the sum is not trivial at all.'

In lockdown, I rediscovered the power of this connection like never before. It was a visceral realization. Every two-minute chat with M from the cafe, or Eddie walking his dog, sent me on my way with a small surge of joy in my heart. For all the isolation of lockdown, I was reminded in those moments that I was rooted in a local community that I knew – and drew immense strength from.

We need these moments of contact that bind us into each other. Our need for other humans is so strong in fact that the effects of loneliness produce signals in the brain very like those of acute hunger. The researchers who discovered this in a 2020 MIT study theorize that it serves as a biological warning system – for humans, loneliness equals danger. Isolation is a growing problem: only 53 per cent of Americans report that they have daily meaningful interactions with other people; 43 per cent feel isolated from others. And Gen Z are the loneliest generation – in the UK, the Office for National Statistics reports that 16–24-year-olds are more lonely than pensioners. The problem is such that the government has appointed a Minister for Loneliness.

The late psychiatrist and broadcaster Dr Anthony Clare had seven rules for happiness, the second of which was 'Be a leaf on a tree'. And the explanation (by the broadcaster Gyles Brandreth, who turned Dr Clare's rules for happiness into a book) beautifully sums up the value of community: 'To thrive, you have to be both an individual – with a sense that you are unique and that you matter – and at the same time you need to be connected to a bigger organism: a family, a community, a company, a club. You need to be part of something bigger than yourself.'

As a side note, it's worth mentioning that connections are the best conduit to genuine diversity and inclusivity. When people spend time with other people in person, prejudices melt away.

We've heard it a lot in recent months but the pandemic really did ignite an appreciation of the community that lies on our doorstep. We were thrown back on to the most local of resources: parks down the road, the walk to the shops, our postie on his rounds.

It's not a surprise that local high streets fared better than city centres during this time. But my strong hunch is that our connection to local isn't going to disappear the minute we are free of restrictions. More than a third (36 per cent) of people in Britain predict that they will keep up their increased use of independent local shops when lockdown ends. Structural changes to how we work will also impact: 74 per cent of UK businesses plan on maintaining some level of home working into the future.

But, most importantly, we've realized the worth of the local: 57 per cent of people intend to keep using shops that offer locally produced goods after lockdown has finished.

In Milan, the mayor is trialling the idea of the

'fifteen-minute city'. This follows an urban planning model from a professor at the Sorbonne, which imagines a city where everything would be accessible within a fifteen-minute walk or cycle. Every neighbourhood would contain enough to fulfil all the functions of life – healthcare, work, education – without the need for a busy and stressful commute. It is about adjusting the rhythms of life, cutting out the dead time spent on station platforms or at bus stops. It is a model that actively takes human wellbeing – rather than just human productivity – into account. It rethinks what a city could be. It's a shift towards localism, and away from the commute to centralized offices, which has been accelerated by the pandemic.

Why do I tell you all this? Not because I want everybody to open a shop on their local high street (though please do your shopping there!). It's to open your eyes to our human need for community, because that should be a foundation of all successful business. Remember the principles: the Kindness Economy asks that we move away from individualist ambition, and towards a broader community vision. Community and connections: they are both an engine for your business and a measure of its true meaningful value.

Communities without limits

Not that community has to mean the streets on your doorstep, of course. The lockdown gave me a fresh appreciation for my own neighbourhood. But it also made me think harder about what community is, and there is a paradox here. On the one hand, lockdown led us to lean heavily on the local. But, on the other, the ease of the digital space allowed us to seek out different tribes completely unhindered by physical boundaries.

It's a larger playing field on which to go about finding community and connection, your place in the world. As lockdowns forced us into unnatural isolation, we reached out for each other in whatever ways we could, and discovered that, in the online space, opportunities were almost endless.

Think of the online yoga classes, attended by people from Aberdeen to Plymouth. The Daybreaker online house parties, virtual classes in stand-up or Latin jazz, the gatherings of charity volunteers working out how best to serve people in need. There was no end to the inventiveness of ordinary people taking their passions online, on scales that ranged from the tiny to the worldwide. We had local art projects for kids, and also the Getty Museum inviting people to recreate their favourite paintings with whatever materials they had to hand. (Kudos to everyone for the inventive use of saucepans and loo rolls in the pursuit of art.) Parents became oh-so-familiar with Joe Wicks's front room (and the occasional breaking of wind) as they huffed and puffed along to his workouts in tandem with hundreds of thousands of people across the world. In looking for people to connect with, we only had to type the right words into our search engines and the world opened up online.

Community is not just about your immediate locale, and the availability of different communities we can engage with will only get more powerful as Gen Z comes of age. For them, looking for their tribes in the virtual space is just as natural as in the physical one. Youth brands built around gaming, livestreaming and social media tend to understand this instinctively. But what happened over lockdown is that others followed them: even those not so digitally savvy found it ever more natural to seek what they wanted online.

In advertising terms, it's the progression that has happened since the so-called 'golden age' when ads went out to one, massive, clearly defined audience. Every time *Corrie* stopped for a few minutes, the viewers who didn't nip off to make a cup of tea would passively consume what was put in front of them and decide to buy or not to buy. Depending on your age, you probably have a 'greatest hits' of these ads in your head – from the Smash robots to the Levi's laundrette to the Milk Tray man. (Or my particular kitsch favourite: the Ferrero Rocher ambassador who spoiled us.)

After that came the age of more active 'users', who chose what they wanted to engage with and on what platform. The advertisers had to find ever more clever ways to reach them.

Today, the really successful brands, especially those aimed at the youth market, have evolved beyond targeting customers. They have followers, not customers; people who engage with them in a fresh dialogue, an eye-to-eye interaction with a whole community. The brand enables the dialogue and sits in the middle of that community, rather than standing above and apart from it.

Only connect

This shifting concept of community has profound implications for business. We have seen time and time again that the brands who are winning are the ones that make people feel that they are part of something larger.

This again is the difference between buying *from* and buying *into*.

The key to this from the brands' perspective is ensuring that people feel part of something greater than a simple purchasing transaction. On the most basic level, it's about making sure that people – whether online or in the physical space – enjoy their interaction with you. (As many as 73 per cent of consumers consider customer experience an important factor in their purchasing decisions, and indeed 42 per cent will actually pay more for a friendly, welcoming experience.)

But this is about far more than basic customer satisfaction. Seth Godin, the author and entrepreneur, memorably puts it this way: 'People do not buy goods and services. They buy relations, stories and magic.' To which I would add, increasingly they buy a sense of community also. And if that community is an active contributor, is doing some good in the world, then so much the better.

It all starts with a conversation. Think of it as the life-enhancing chat at your local butcher's till writ large – with the rules of engagement as important as they are face to face.

Targeted content, for instance, can become an onslaught. Nobody wants to be bombarded with ads for the pair of slippers they looked at once. Or have their email clogged with messages from a company they last bought from in 2010. Being shouted at only increases people's sense of disconnection from a business. Flooding people with content that's clearly delivered via algorithms, trying to trigger nothing more than the buying impulse, simply drains the interaction of conviviality. (Which accounts for the fact that mobile ad blocking rose globally by 64 per cent between 2016 and 2019.)

Instead, brands need to foster a sense of starting a wider, interesting, more free-ranging conversation that the customer can join if they choose. Vibrant successful brands that cater to the youth market know all this instinctively. Take Rihanna's Fenty makeup line, Supreme, or the Phluid Project. Buying from them feels like you are opting into something bigger than just the item in your basket. They galvanize conversation via their social platforms. Their shops are social hubs providing a space where their communities can flourish.

Supreme's stores feature a layout specifically designed for people to skate in; the Phluid Project hosts events and promotes discussion; Fenty excels in the online space, encouraging its followers to post pictures and become part of the visible face of the brand.

Two-way interaction – between business and customer – is transformed into something deeper and broader: by weaving a net of community and connecting members of it with each other, businesses set in motion a conversation that moves far beyond the boundaries of a simple selling proposition.

Strength in community

Successful businesses are growing because of the power of community. Community equals connection, and we all crave connection in our lives.

Take Glossier: perhaps one of the most famous market disruptors of recent years. The billion-dollar company was born out of a blog started in 2010 by founder Emily Weiss. She was employed at *Vogue* during the day and working on 'Into the Gloss' from 4am to 7am, building a community of hundreds of thousands of beauty aficionados.

In 2014 she used this platform to launch four products under the Glossier.com name, inspired by the gaps in the market she had identified through her blog and the conversations on it. Of the twelve venture capital companies she approached, eleven turned her down. The twelfth – run by a woman, Kirsten Green – has had her faith handsomely repaid.

What Glossier did was to create a dialogue – a symbiotic

relationship between the business and the people it serves. It's not just about selling them cosmetics; it's about giving them contact and connections. The brand creates the forum and the value system, and the community rallies around that.

This was live-action interplay between brand and customer: Glossier set up a Slack channel, for its 1,000 most dedicated customers to provide feedback and contribute ideas. It asked its customers what their dream cleanser would be like *before* launching the first range. It created a love for the brand, and a sense of ownership, right from the start.

All of this has led to Glossier becoming a so-called 'unicorn' – a privately owned company worth $1 billion or more. Even more interesting is the fact that the Glossier model has completely disrupted the power of the old beauty corporations – behemoths that were used to having the playing field to themselves.

This all tells us how businesses can use the power of community to flourish. What is even more interesting is how by doing so brands actually contribute to the Kindness Economy. Done right, it can be a beautiful symbiosis.

In much the same way, BrewDog uses its 'Equity for Punks' scheme to draw on the community they have built not only to crowdfund, but to tap into their passions and knowledge. What better example of the bridge between community and business than a company that asks its followers for informed suggestions about where they might set up their next bar, or what they want to see in the next launch? But more than that – as we shall see later on, they have used the power built up through community actively to push their values, and to give back.

Remember Sirine and Matt, who took the challenges thrown at them by the pandemic and opened up an ice-cream bar? The further lovely twist to their story comes with the knowledge that when they set up their shop – in the teeth of adversity – they made a conscious decision to actively support the beleaguered freelance theatre workforce by employing them. Consequently, says Sirine, 'the freelance theatre community helped us by adapting what *they* normally did. A prolific theatre designer tiled our beautiful bar. A renowned theatre props mistress helped us make our sign.' It became a beautiful illustration of community in action, where the community feeds the brand, which in turn gives back to the community and to the wider world.

Nike feeds back into its roots through its Community Stores: shops they have opened in deprived areas where there is a strong emphasis on the local neighbourhood. The most recent is in Watts, Los Angeles. Some 85 per cent of the staff in these shops are hired from within three miles of the store, employees are paid to give hours to local community projects, and an employee-led grants programme funnels money into supporting local organizations. Local talent is celebrated, and the whole branding of the shop champions its locale.

It's not all one-way traffic. For a brand that needs to stay relevant to a young streetwise audience, a direct line to the talent and creative energy of the community they serve is invaluable. And, fantastic model though it is, Nike currently has only eight Community Stores in the US out of a total of over 7,000 outlets worldwide. But it's something and it's a start. Let's hope they roll this concept out in order to fully, and meaningfully, embody it.

Community forms a key pillar of the Kindness Economy. Not just because drawing on the human need for connection will help power a business to success – although it will – but because the community vision gives you the chance to build something meaningful. There is a beautiful loop here: businesses working with the power of community to build themselves in strength and meaning, and in turn feeding back in a measure of wellbeing, heart and soul which sustains a wider, more meaningful purpose.

Humans need to connect. It's what we do. Each small, seemingly trivial connection – whether it's online, or a conversation at the till, or the flash of recognition that comes from a brand we love – is a small spark. It's the job of businesses to nurture those sparks, kindle them into tiny fires. If you do that, those flames can be both a beacon, welcoming our community, and a hearth, enhancing our lives.

TO DO

Always listening, always learning

Communities start with conversations.

Of course, conduct research. Of course, talk to your customers and look at what influencers have to say.

What we find interesting is less the influencer, more the witness – the people listening and hearing all the time, engaged on the front line. Never underestimate the power of someone on a checkout till or in a fitting room to give you valuable info on why a product was liked or not liked.

From my own experience I know that some of the best CEOs in the game visit their stores day in and day out. These are the ones who listen and know who to surround themselves with. The same goes for a good office manager, a good colleague. In fact, it goes for us as good neighbours, good friends, good parents.

This is where your community starts – with your own people.

9

Where's Your Creative Instinct?

The great Carl Jung once wrote: 'Your vision will become clear only when you can look into your heart. Who looks outside, dreams. Who looks inside, awakens.'

For me, this idea of heart and vision can be summed up in one concept: creative instinct.

This is a time of reimagining. The way we work is changing, we have a chance to redefine business in the interests of humanity – and it's a liberating feeling. Remember – these are the plastic hours, when we have the opportunity to mould what comes next. The future is exciting, but full of unknowns, and when we're in uncharted territory, creative instinct is our best compass. It guides us in a unique way so that we are not distracted by external forces, or the sometimes very negative impact of our own internal dialogues. It's pure. It's elemental. It's a gut feeling.

I once talked to Sharmadean Reid, the very inspirational founder of WAH Nails and Beautystack, about what creativity and intuition meant to her, and how she had harnessed those powers. She described it very simply: 'I feel like I've always had an inkling for the future.' Now, that is pretty singular, and not many people have that surefire instinct. But it illustrates how great businesses founded on instinct can forge new paths.

Something else she said also resonated: 'Strong companies and strong founders create markets that didn't exist before, and that's very difficult to comprehend if you don't think like that.' Exactly. This gut instinct can be hard to get across in the boardroom. How do you explain an 'inkling for the future', when all that the data and figures can show you is the past? To be strong in business, we need to learn to listen to our gut, and not allow it to be drowned out by data, or systems, or numbers, or the limited thinking of other people.

I was very young when I was promoted to director at Harvey Nichols. I got the job essentially because of the creativity, risk and ideas I kept producing. I didn't work to any grand vision. I listened to my gut, I felt what was right for the brand – how to make it buzzy and talked about and vibrant. My instinct led me, and it was a huge success.

I was made a board member because I was able to let my creativity flourish, but the minute they put me on the board it changed. I found myself playing a corporate role. I had to listen to and be defined by the figures, and from the moment I found myself sitting in the boardroom having to back up my decisions with numbers and data and projections, I lost my instinct. I lost my ability to take risks. I lost who I was. And so Harvey Nichols lost me.

Creativity is in everybody. It's a human instinct. And we are at grave risk if we continue to silence it in business as we have. Relying solely on data or on past performance metrics to make our decisions, we can end up with businesses and systems that are nothing but ever paler photocopies of the original. Pushing everything through a funnel of financial fear – and never-ending growth – risks hampering the kind of experimentation that's vital to our businesses.

Too many companies today are copyists that lack creativity

at their heart. Think of the cookie-cutter chains of lacklustre restaurants filling our high streets. Think of the fashion brands whose clothes and ethos are indistinguishable from the shop next door. The identikit companies that sell us home insurance or mortgages, all cheery graphics up front on their webpages, but impenetrable to anything that doesn't fit their algorithms.

These bland businesses, hanging all their identity on one peg, are rooted in the fear of failing. Without creativity to guide them, they are stuck with looking in the rear-view mirror, reliant on data and numbers and what has worked before for someone else.

Fear hamstrings creativity. And the vital financial element of the business world can sadly allow this fear to flourish all too easily. The academic and advisor on education Ken Robinson, in his seminal 2006 TED talk, reflected on how the stymying of creativity for children at school impacts the way we do business as adults. '[Kids are] not frightened of being wrong . . . if you're not prepared to be wrong, you'll never come up with anything original . . . And by the time they get to be adults, most kids have lost that capacity. They have become frightened of being wrong. And we run our companies like this. We stigmatize mistakes.'

Creative instinct is empathetic at the core. And this is where your community vision should come into play. Identifying your people, defining who you are talking to and why, boldly calling out to them: that is where the creative conversation lies, and it frees you from the tyranny of trying to be all things to all men. It's about thinking deeply about what people need, how to solve problems for them, or create a relationship with them and how this will make them feel – whether that's externally or internally in your organization. The really great businesses are the ones that instinctively understand people.

Numbers are, of course, a key part of business, but they cannot be allowed to dictate every aspect of it. This has been one liberation that sprang out of the chaos of the pandemic. With life as we knew it stripped back, we entered a place whose boundaries we did not know. There was no relying on projections or Q1 targets when all that had been ripped up and thrown out the window. In this land of dragons, we had nothing to lose and almost accidentally abandoned the fear of getting it 'wrong'. It gave rise to a flourishing of truly original thinking.

When the pandemic hit, creativity became a necessity. We lost all the certainties we were used to. Targets, balance sheets and quarterly predictions were blown out of the water. What was left was our intuition, underpinned by empathy. There was no time for fear – and many used their creative instinct to experiment and adapt in unknowable times. More than ever, creativity has to be part of our arsenal for survival: we cannot continue to operate with systems so rigid they throttle the human out of us.

We know the economic weather ahead is worse than uncertain. Storms are coming, and navigating these storms is going to need courage. Drawing on what we have learned in the past year will give us that. An Australian survey by Xero found that over 50 per cent of businesses that have thrived over the pandemic pointed at gut instinct as the main thing they relied on to get them through. Thrivers, the survey points out, are more willing to self-invent.

When times are as hard as this, we can't look back at past performance to see us through. Our standard metrics aren't up to the job. Data alone is not going to cut it. The new way that we will be living requires a whole new approach to understanding the world, and a whole new suite of questions about how to operate within it.

The physics and the chemistry

I believe we've reached a tipping point, when the past few decades' prioritization of ever more sophisticated operations will start to be rebalanced with an increased appreciation of the critical value of creative instinct. It's about better integrating the *physics* of businesses – how to produce things and deliver them without friction – with the *chemistry* – the subtle magic that elevates a business into something greater.

We will not, of course, sacrifice the physics. We need technology and all the advantages it offers us. But as tech evangelist Ben Southworth said several years ago, technology could give us back the freedom to recover our humanity: as more and more processes become mechanized, 'The days of unskilled manual labour exchanged for money will gradually be gone, reserved for the very few, and this opens up a raft of opportunities for us to be engaged in more meaningful, thoughtful, contemplative, compassionate and creative work. As a consequence, we will become more humane, more human.'

Jack Ma, co-founder of Alibaba Group, one of the world's most successful businesses, is another who pinpoints creativity as the most important attribute for the future. Speaking at the World Economic Forum in 2018, he emphasized the importance of teaching creativity to our future generations – it is this, he believes, that will provide the edge in an increasingly technological world. Where machines grow ever smarter, they do not grow wiser, so he believes education should prioritize the skills of creativity, humanity, wisdom and 'being human' in an age of artificial intelligence.

The mother of invention

At its heart, creativity stems from resourcefulness. It's not necessarily about blue-sky thinking, or dreaming up unusual ideas. Often, creativity comes through the open-minded search for solutions, a practical, optimistic application to a problem.

We've seen a wealth of this kind of thinking during the past year, as during the pandemic businesses, people and communities have responded to events and come up with ideas on how to survive economically and practically, as well as connect emotionally.

I think of KC Roasters in Mumbai, turning its roastery and warehouse into a logistics hub through its Shop Local scheme, so that its staff could pack and ship goods from local businesses. I think of my favourite local restaurant in London, which, unable to make the business work with social distancing rules, put up cabins on the street to serve people, instituted a membership scheme, and completely revitalized the business into something rather wonderful. I think of ex-footballer Lou Macari, who runs a homeless shelter. Forced to close it down because Covid restrictions prevented people sleeping in dormitories, he had the brainwave of installing wooden glamping pods inside a warehouse. It turned out to be a transformative idea – not least, thinks Macari, because with all the pods being separately numbered, the residents each had their own singular address, a godsend for job applications.

Above all, I think of my visit to Lord's cricket ground to

get my Covid vaccine. It was the complete transformation of the venue that struck me: all the hard-won fast thinking that had turned a massive sporting venue, more used to accommodating hordes of cheering fans, into a perfectly flowing, user-friendly medical facility. This wasn't a top-down design process: it had been put together by people on the ground working within the constraints of what they had. It wasn't showy, it wasn't artistic or aesthetically pleasing in any way, but it was a practical, resourceful, hands-on drive to get the most vital thing done. And it was being replicated in thousands of places up and down the country. There was something moving about that: it felt like a machine for joy.

This is what I think about when I think about creativity: the flowering of something huge from tiny seeds, reliant on ingenuity, human endeavour and the willingness to push through difficulties.

Finding your instinct

Relax. You don't need to turn yourself into Elon Musk overnight. Not every leader will be brimful of creative instinct themselves. But it's certainly true that a great leader will know how to foster it throughout the whole of their organization. I want to move away from thinking of creativity as being just about zhuzhing up the way the business presents itself.

Our concept of creativity has narrowed to the extent that it's often siloed to one department or, even worse, a 'creative' agency full of people equipped with hipster beards and cold brew. The need for creative instinct – and the people who have it – extends into every area of a business, from product to packaging to the systems of the organization itself. It's an environment, a culture, that every member of the business can foster. And this is exactly how we at Portas partner with businesses – we don't just give teams creative ideas and disappear; we arm them with the confidence to co-create them and make them actually happen – together.

Creating a culture throughout the whole business in which people can truly express themselves and their ideas in turn creates limitless possibilities. I love Sophia Loren's response when she was asked in a *Desert Island Discs* interview what it was like working with Vittorio De Sica, who directed her in *Two Women*, one of her first great roles.

'He really helped you believe in yourself, didn't he?' asks the interviewer.

Sophia lets a beat go by before she answers. 'When I was working with him, I didn't have to believe in myself – I *was* myself.'

When our jobs empower us to be ourselves, to bring all the kindness, compassion and empathy that we manifest in our daily lives into our work, then creative instinct has the oxygen it needs to flourish.

So much of our collective ability to rebuild will hinge on our individual ability to imagine a better world and paint its contours into existence, and we need the pure force that is creative instinct to guide us. Over the past year, so many of us have seen the world in greyscale: our conversations muffled by masks and a feeling of liquid fear (and collective grief) numbing our senses.

The buzzing, blooming life-force of creativity is the counterpoint to all this. It's this essence that will power businesses and give them the competitive edge they need to thrive. Hang on to this essence, don't lose it, because it is the future.

It's not a tool you bring out in times of crisis. It is the life-blood that will not only energize your business, but energize humanity.

As the urbanist Richard Florida argues in his book *The Rise of the Creative Class*, 'human creativity is the ultimate economic resource'. I believe that idea has never been more relevant.

TO DO

Be curious

Creative instinct is well-trained intuition. This intuition takes the listening and the learning that are at the heart of creating a community, and transforms them into ideas.

For this to work, it's crucial to build structures in which creative conversations can flow.

● Be alert to finding new ways of doing things, because habit is the enemy of creativity. Curiosity is the channel through which you find your way.

● Take inspiration from as many places as possible. Go as broad as you can. What you're passionate about can inspire you in your work life. Don't disconnect your work from what you love – be it literature, poetry, music, sport . . .

● Can you allocate 10 per cent of your budget to R&D?

● Use the online space meaningfully. We talk about doom-scrolling. Curate your scroll so it becomes nourishing and you're walking through inspiration. In a world of Google/ Amazon/curated social feeds, there's no serendipity. You exist in an echo chamber. How can you burst that bubble? Creativity needs this. How do you create serendipity? Allow time to wander, get lost, pause 'productivity' for a while and embrace free thinking.

● Listen to all the voices you can within your organization because that is how ideas come. Conversation, the sharing of knowledge, reflecting on and developing this knowledge – this in itself is a creative process. Walking the shop floor, in business, is an auditing exercise. In life, figure out where your floor stretches to and walk it. I always carry a leather folder with a notebook, and I've noticed that all the people I talk to have different ways of archiving things that inspire them, from Instagram to a digital notebook to a folder of pictures on your phone.

Give yourself permission to use this inspiration, and give yourself permission for it not to work. Yes, it's uncomfortable. But this is how you learn and progress.

10

The Kindness Economy in Action

We've seen a lot of theory throughout this book. But what does it feel like to put that theory into action? I know what my own journey has been like – tough at times, always invigorating, bloody worthwhile. But I wanted to talk to leaders from other businesses – new, established, big, small, at different stages of their journey – about how they took these ideas out of abstraction and into the actual cut and thrust of the business world.

Here are their stories.

Sheep Inc. – fashioning a new path

Sheep Inc. is a new knitwear brand that has its roots firmly in its founder's principles. The company is small, but has at its heart a gigantic ambition: to change the way we buy and think about fashion.

This is a second business for co-founder Edzard van der Wyck. His previous venture was the very successful Heist Studios, which revolutionized the way tights were made. That experience gave him first-hand insight into the devastating impact the fashion industry was having on the environment (as well as a track record in reimagining a product from the ground up). It made him start to ask the fundamental questions about what legacy he would be leaving behind, not least because it was around this time that he had his first child – 'a generational thinking starts to seep into your being', he says.

His new business therefore started with a question that had begun to resonate deep inside him: 'How do you hold the fashion industry to account? And how do you implement a new business model that could pave a new way forward?'

That – pretty large – question was where it all began for Edzard and his co-founders Michael Wessely and Gavin Erasmus. It's a question that is squarely in Kindness Economy territory: spot the 'and' in there. This is the additive space: don't just build a brand that minimizes its own impact; build a brand that cuts a new path for others to follow.

Working with a think-tank, the Copenhagen Institute of Interaction Design, he researched the question of why people weren't necessarily buying sustainable fashion. (This was in 2017 – he points out that things have already changed in a few short years: gradually, then suddenly, remember.)

Central to his thinking was the 'them/us' question of how consumers and producers intersect, especially in fashion. As he puts it, we have become conditioned to think about what we are putting into our bodies; we eat organic, we now think about the impact on the planet of foodstuffs that are produced unsustainably. 'But when it comes to fashion, which is the stuff we put on top of our body, we're not conditioned to ask that question. We just pick something up, try it on, we like it and we then go pay for it.' So how could he get more people to start thinking about the clothes that they buy?

With that core-deep question established, his next questions rippled outwards: 'Now, conceptually, what should a business tomorrow look like? How does it behave? How does it operate? How does it source materials? How does it treat manufacturing, how does it treat aftercare? We really interrogated every single part of the business to try to figure out what it is that we would need to do to implement change today.'

An advantage was that Michael Wessely came from a background of finance, not fashion, which gave him an outsider's perspective on the received wisdoms of the industry.

In fashion, the fickle tides of taste and style work to contradict the sustainable ambition. The business needed to find a way to be impervious to fashion trends. Picturing black-and-white photos of Ernest Hemingway in a big rollneck sweater, and realizing that he was still wearing his own father's old jumpers, Edzard realized that knitwear could have this design permanence.

Having landed on knitwear, the next step was to look very carefully at what materials they might use. Merino wool was the best fit for longevity, quality and impact. But merino wool can come with sourcing issues and with environmental problems in its processing, all of which would have to be overcome.

The first question was how to ensure the raw material was as sustainable as possible. Edzard and his business partners did this by turning the sourcing process on its head. The normal supply chain distances the brand from the raw material as a matter of course: brand goes to manufacturer, manufacturer goes to yarn mill, yarn mill goes to scour wool broker, and on down the chain, with a layer of opacity at every stage and little control over what is being supplied. Sheep Inc. reversed this by starting with the source – the farms – from the outset.

If they could pick the right farms – ones with a positive

environmental impact – then they could follow the wool through the whole process. They worked with a group called ZQ Merino, and identified three New Zealand farms that were 'really pushing the boundaries on land management', allowing them to sequester more CO_2 than they produced, as well as having impeccable animal welfare standards.

This forensic attention was repeated right through the supply process. The discovery of a factory in Germany that was pushing material science means they use a chlorine-free method called eternity treatment that results in a softer, more durable yarn. The factory, naturally, uses regenerative energy. The knitting is done at a carbon-neutral knitting facility on Japanese knitting machines 'which are amazing, they look like giant printers, and they kind of print the sweater. And that means that it's totally seamless.'

The result is knitwear that is not only carbon negative – the Sheep Inc. website carries a tracker of how much carbon the company sequesters – but that builds in radical transparency as a matter of course. Each jumper carries a Near Field Communication (NFC) tag that allows the buyer to trace its journey right back to the individual sheep (and to get updates on how that sheep is doing). The company invests 5 per cent of its revenue into biodiversity projects.

This is interconnectedness in action – a care for how every stage of the process impacts on the world.

But interconnectedness is not the only Kindness Economy principle that Sheep Inc. embodies. Their story shows the Kindness Economy principles woven into the fabric of the brand. This is a business with philosophy – how can I make a difference to this industry? – at its core. The brand's values run through everything they do. Community and creativity come together in the regular 'Wouldn't it be cool if . . .'

meetings which give everyone in the company a voice and generate future ideas for the business.

Edzard is clearly quite a whizz at the hard and soft skills also, understanding that a 'work work work' culture does nobody any good, while accepting the tough realities of being an entrepreneur. In his first business he used to feel he had to be in the office till 10pm – 'just doing it because that's what you're supposed to do'. Now, he is much more about balance: 'We want internally to show how you can set up a business in a positive way – I'd like to think that we're nice guys as well,' and he makes an interesting point about sacrifice: 'I think this idea of sacrifice is also a really dangerous word – that somehow you need to sacrifice some success of the business by working less.' It's certainly refreshing, and great, to see these more progressive working practices modelled by a man . . .

Edzard sees the process of bringing about change as operating on two levels: ambitious purpose and continual tweaks: 'You start with a purpose – to be a fashion brand of tomorrow. That doesn't mean we have to solve it today. It has to remain a continuous drive and ambition to be always moving in that direction . . . Continuously interrogate what you're doing, and understand that it's a journey, not a destination.

'You can never do enough because you want to do better. But you can also never do enough because you always need to be the most innovative brand out there.'

He sees a mind shift happening in the post-Covid landscape, an increasing awareness of the impact of the choices we make – 'the buy less, buy better' mindset.

As for what he's most proud of? 'The way the brand has resonated in the market. It's been hugely positive, because you see how much change is starting to take place.'

It's a small revolution perhaps, but a meaningful one. The industry is taking notice – Sheep Inc. won a Drapers Sustainable Fashion Award in 2021 for Best Supply Chain Initiative, up against the titans of H&M and Marks & Spencer.

What if this level of accountability became the gold standard across the industry? What a revolution that would be.

Unilever – a giant undertaking

From the small to the giant. It's one thing to implement business practices hinged on values and ethics in a new start-up, but is there a similar desire to make change with enormous, established businesses at the other end of the scale? Unilever is one of the world's biggest household goods companies and the largest company on the FTSE 100 index. These are the people who make your laundry powder, your toothpaste, your jars of Marmite, your teabags, the bleach you put down your loo . . . The list goes on.

So imagine how quickly my ears pricked up when I turned on my radio in January 2021 to hear the CEO of this behemoth announcing a raft of new policies designed to help build a fairer and more inclusive society. The keystone of this is a commitment to make sure everyone who provides goods or services to the company earns at least a fair living wage – not the minimum wage, but a fair living wage – by 2030.

This is the latest step Unilever has taken in support of climate action and sustainability, and it goes along with two other key strategic initiatives: to spend €2 billion annually with suppliers owned and managed by under-represented groups, and to pioneer new employment models. They are aiming for net zero carbon from their own operations by 2030, and net zero across their whole supply chain by 2039.

In other words, they are putting their money where their mouth is.

'Everything we do through our business and our brands must be underpinned by an absolute commitment to respect human rights,' says CEO Alan Jope in the company's Human Rights Report of 2020. (In itself, this document is a pretty hefty commitment to the concept of transparency in business.) This isn't bandwagon-jumping: Unilever's Sustainable Living Plan was put in place by Alan Jope's predecessor, Paul Polman. One of Polman's initiatives, interestingly, was to scrap short-term targets within the business. Jope has taken the baton and is running with it.

Alan Jope's words on Radio 4's *Today* programme that morning resonated – just look back at the table of Kindness Economy principles, and see how they square up with his perspective. He identifies the rise of what he calls 'conscious consumption', especially in the wake of the pandemic, and wholeheartedly believes that values firmly rooted in social responsibility 'is *definitely* going to become a reason for people to preferentially choose our brands'.

He also spoke about the wider picture: 'A society where everyone makes a fair living wage is a society where people have the money to spend on clothing, feeding, educating themselves, and that's good for business.' Most of all, he says, 'Without healthy societies, we don't have a healthy business.'

As you would expect from a company operating at this level, he is presenting the thinking behind this new strategy not as fluffy idealizing, but as commercially savvy strategy. This is social responsibility going hand in hand with financial profitability.

At a Reuters Next event in 2021, Jope spoke about the priorities of the company. What he said could have been a direct description of the Kindness Economy's 'rippling out' effect. 'Our first priority is our employees,' he said. 'Then we take care of our customers and consumers, our business partners, the planet, the societies we do business in – when we do all these things well, our shareholders will be very well rewarded. We do not believe in a shareholder primacy model.'

All of which made me intrigued enough to want to talk to the company about how they saw businesses with purpose taking on the challenge of social responsibility.

Aline Santos, executive VP of global marketing, is hugely proud of the company purpose to make sustainable living commonplace. It is something that is reflected globally across Unilever's brands, and in Aline's own work: she was involved in the first advertising in the Brazilian market to feature Black women as protagonists. She worked on the groundbreaking Dove Real Beauty campaign, which famously featured realistic and real women in its advertisements, and on the Dirt is Good campaign for Persil, which put experiential learning and children's wellbeing at the heart of its marketing.

People, humanity, lie at the heart of things for Aline, just as they do for me. 'To break down stereotypes and help people feel included with a deep sense of belonging' is her own personal driver. It's encapsulated in Unilever's Unstereotype movement – which set a global aim of moving advertising away from gender stereotyping across all its brands. Again, this is collaborative, regenerative work, which they share with everyone, including their competitors, through the Unstereotype Alliance, launched in conjunction with UN Women and other industry leaders in 2017.

For Aline, the responsibility of businesses to work for the greater good is not in question: 'You only need to look at the major societal challenges of last year [2020] to see that the battle against systemic bias in society today has never been more urgent. Brands and advertisers have a huge role to play in shaping culture, and as an industry we must work to accelerate solutions to solve one of the world's biggest challenges – inclusion.'

It's an attitude that seems to be shared across the whole company, from the top downwards. If they achieve all their goals – and, even better, if their example paves the way for others to follow in their footsteps – the effects could be massive.

Lush – compassionate creativity

Mark Constantine is CEO and co-founder of Lush cosmetics, a pioneering company that has taken a corner of the cosmetics industry and turned it on its head. From ingredients, to packaging, to the way it connects with its customers, Lush has always placed ethical considerations – and in particular animal rights – at the heart of the business. It works to an ethical charter, is co-owned by employees and has taken knocks to its bottom line in order to introduce socially progressive initiatives. All of which has propelled it to enormous success – in 2017 it had a turnover of £995 million, with nearly a thousand shops worldwide.

Mark is a rebel in lots of ways, a capitalist with a conscience, happy to describe himself as a hippy. He and his company are absolutely all about doing the right thing by the planet. But he's also an entrepreneur to his bones and told it straight when I talked to him for my *Kindness Economy* podcast: 'I like making profit.'

He is a businessman through and through, but doesn't see a contradiction between this and having a social conscience: 'Everything we can do, we should do.' Uncaring business practices are nowadays 'not sustainable and not sensible, and will upset people's profits, and will upset their commercial enterprise. And that's why it's such an exciting time now.'

I wanted to ask him where he felt the values of the company sprang from. For a start, he said he didn't much like Lush being called an 'ethical business' – though they certainly are. 'I just think most people, when they work here, just see that as normal.'

He went on: 'The weird thing is that in business, what we learned in school pretty much works, doesn't it? Try not to copy anyone, try to be quite nice to each other, try to get along . . . And then when you come out to business, suddenly that's not normal business. Normal business is something less pleasant than that.

'I can't see the point of the lying, the cheating, the manipulating. I don't know where it gets me. I'm keen to win. But I don't see that it gets me to the win.'

From top to bottom, the company is full of initiatives that find the additive, generative space: 'Recreating a dynamic environment, greening the desert, replacing sterile areas with fecund and lush places . . . the more that things are vital and vibrant, the more exciting the opportunities to make profit become,' Mark told me, in a nice evocation of the 'me and we' principle.

Whether it is sourcing the salt for their bath bombs from salt pans that will help preserve migratory birds (and keep traditional employment afloat), or going to great lengths to ensure that the essential oils they use have a transparent and ethical supply chain, Lush's sustainable credentials infuse the brand as much as their signature scents infuse the atmosphere of their stores. They have made it part of their USP, and customers love them for it.

For Mark, business is all about the balance between rational business and values passion. Mark's favourite poet is Kahlil Gibran, who speaks of reason and passion being the rudder and sails of your seafaring soul. In order to successfully navigate, you need both: the steadying force of core business principles to create the rudder that steers your organization, and the wind of passion to make it speed along.

How does he approach change in a company that is already radical in its approach? In small steps or as one grand vision? 'Both: what I do is gather lots of opinions. I don't have a lot of opinions of my own.'

Even for a purpose-driven brand like Lush, the grand vision can be hard. About five years ago, Mark jokes, he took himself away to try to thrash out a plan. The task of trying to put together a detailed strategy proved beyond him, though: 'I couldn't do it. I just couldn't do it. I couldn't make it all work. Then, eventually, just stealing from Elon Musk, I just did this very simple plan, which was: "Be number one in every market. A product for every need. Start a cosmetics revolution."' A pretty huge ambition, especially when it had to be underpinned by the ethical values that Lush embodies. But actually it has served him well. The products he launches do tend to go shooting to the forefront of the market. A broad-brush approach has worked for him, but it's notable that he keeps a careful track of the detail too: at the time I spoke to him he was in daily contact with his team about how the brand's mascara was doing.

He's realistic about change, though: 'People hate it, don't they?' he says ruefully. What makes me laugh is that every time I talk to Mark about his business, he reflexively brings it back to the people he works with, while still maintaining that he is all about the product: 'The vision and the culture of my business is provided by the people within it.' Those who work at Lush tend to be very driven by values – a lot of vegans, apparently – and he has a great description of the people he's surrounded by: 'People who care so much are fiercely kind. Compassionate.'

So perhaps I shouldn't have been surprised when I asked Mark what he was most proud of. I thought he might hit me with a huge sustainability goal they have achieved, or the innovations they have introduced into the cosmetics industry. Instead, he pointed to Lush's maternity benefit: 'I worked with another colleague on the maternity benefit. She was going to go off to have a baby and she dreamed up the best maternity benefit she could, I agreed it and we doubled the number of babies every year in Lush. A lot of women work for us, so if they feel more secure to have babies, I think we're doing a bloody good job. And I'm very proud of myself.'

That is a true Kindness Economy business: innovative to its fingertips, with humanity at its heart.

BT – connecting through kindness

How do you apply Kindness Economy principles to a national institution like BT – a giant in the telecommunications sector with more than 100,000 employees?

I decided to call Pete Oliver, MD for Small and Medium Enterprise at BT, to find out. I have known Pete for a while as a sponsor of my *Kindness Economy* podcasts, so I know this subject is close to his heart.

I began by asking when, in his opinion, BT started thinking about social responsibility initiatives. 'There has been a good CSR agenda at BT for many years – for instance, years and years ago we moved all of our power to renewable sources,' he told me.

The change that has particularly inspired him, though, came about a few years back: a big digital skills programme targeted both at businesses and ordinary regular consumers that was part of a larger brand refresh. The aim? To help BT customers navigate the digital space.

Within the overarching brand purpose ('We connect for good'), BT set the ambitious target of helping 1 million small business owners and employees with digital skills training. It's about 'a higher purpose rather than we just sell you a broadband connection'.

Note the Kindness Economy 'and' here. This is great news for the businesses themselves, who are given the chance to upskill. It's also good for BT's business. They sell connectivity, so the more their customers become digitally savvy and get more from the BT product, the better. It's not a surprise to hear that the value of this initiative really proved its worth when the pandemic hit in 2020. It meant the framework was in place for BT to move swiftly to help its customers navigate the bewildering new Covid landscape.

The first task was to understand what small businesses would be facing – for this they connected with Small Business Britain, a not-for-profit organization that works with small businesses. The second task was to ramp up the existing investment in developing small business skills, and especially to take it all online. Digital workshops were set up, online mentoring was introduced.

Change in a company as large as BT is a process, not a one-time revolution. This initiative was already in place, and already in tune with the company philosophy, but it needed to accelerate hard when the pandemic hit. Key to success, thinks Pete, is setting a goal 'that people can see is ambitious and meaningful', and then 'getting started and having stages on the way there . . . It's very continuous. We learned a lot from doing this early on about what worked, how you engage people.'

Crucially, this was leader-led, from the CEO down, signalling that this was something that was important for the organization, with a clear goal. There was throughout a message 'that this has got scale, that the CEO was talking about it'. Consistent communication was vital, with regular updates and a willingness to prioritize what worked best (bite-size content and online mentoring).

In an interesting internal and external interconnectivity effect, the online mentoring scheme for small businesses has proved to be something that has really bolstered morale across the whole company. 'What's been great is seeing a lot of BT people at all management levels contribute something back to small business owners.' Hundreds of BT employees have volunteered to take part, Pete included – from all different corners of the company: cybersecurity, or HR, or digital marketing. They give over their time, and in return they are finding a deeper connection to the brand's customers.

This is what Pete points to as the thing he is most proud of. He speaks fondly of the mentoring session he gave to the owner of a small Indian takeaway. 'He'd been doing a brilliant job getting himself online for takeaways and was trying to think through how to do his marketing and how to be less reliant on people like Deliveroo and do his own thing. You suddenly realized this was a guy whose only staff, really, were people working in the kitchen, himself, and a member of his family.'

In giving the takeaway owner some useful advice – how to get listed on Google, how to develop a website with the minimum of investment – Pete found himself learning a lot about BT's customers, and feeling that he had really been able to help. He has seen this replicated again and again across all the volunteers.

All of which is good for BT's overall purpose strategy – always a difficult thing to implement across 100,000 people.

'Tell me honestly,' I asked Pete, 'ten years ago, if some-one had said you were going to be doing all this for free, would it have gone ahead . . . ?'

'It would have been less,' he admits. 'I don't think it would have been on the scale that businesses are doing nowadays.'

The big ongoing commitment to a programme like this is a real signifier of how Kindness Economy principles are embedding themselves into companies of this size.

Why does he think this is?

He points to two reasons: 'First of all, the availability of information on what brands and businesses are doing has never been greater. Any business you want to interact with, whether it's big or small, you can go online, read reviews, find out about alternatives. People's access to information about businesses and what they're doing has really changed even in the last ten years.' (Spot the glass walls, anyone?) That means that 'the expectations of businesses have changed hugely . . . For your customers you've got to do more. You have got to show that you've got more than just a product. You have something bigger that you're doing as a business.'

There you have it in a nutshell: in this new world, what-ever your product is, you have to do more.

I was intrigued also by the second part of Pete's answer, not least because Alan Jope of Unilever has said almost the same thing.

'The expectation of people who work for us – it's partly a generational thing but not only generational – people nowadays want to work for someone with clear purpose, who's doing something more than just being a business making money. To get the best talent nowadays, people ask questions about what does your business stand for, what else are you doing?'

They certainly do. And in the new Kindness Economy landscape, you had better have the answers.

Rapha – community in action

Rapha's roots lie squarely in founder Simon Mottram's love of his sport, cycling. For him, the business 'came out of a passion for the thing, rather than a passion for having a business full stop'.

This isn't bland corporate-speak 'passion': it's deep in Simon's bones. His love for cycling comes down to something ineffable.

'The most important thing to me,' he says, 'is the fact that when I ride my bike, everything makes sense. The world makes sense. So it's physical and mental therapy for me . . . daily therapy, body and mind.'

This is the philosophy of the brand, right at its core.

Rapha grew out of a desire to share with the world the wellbeing that cycling gave Simon. His first step? 'Lots and lots of research . . . The whole thing came from my gut and my personal experience, and I had to work out if I was just this weird loner, or whether there were other people like me.'

The challenge lay in the fact that this was 2004, well before MAMILs were a thing – that's 'middle-aged men in Lycra', in case you're not familiar with the acronym. But you'll certainly have seen a lot of them around. In 2004, cycling was not visible or stylish in the way that it is now, and the idea of it needing a premium sportswear brand was unthinkable – something borne out by the fact that it took Simon 200 meetings to raise the initial £140,000.

Quite something, then, that Simon's aim was to 'make cycling the most popular sport in the world. And it's still the purpose. And it's still our North Star.'

On the way to that North Star, the company identified a number of missions. The first was just about creating a brand which would bring cycling out of its closet, give it the kind of products and cachet and style to make people reflexively think, 'Ah. Cycling's cool.' (Job done on that one, then.)

The second mission was textbook Kindness Economy: 'The second mission was all about building community,' says Simon. 'It was rapha.cc from the start, which means cycle club. So let's start building it as a club, as a community. Let's bring people in and let's support their lives, their cycling lives, with experiences, rides and better products.'

This has been the brand's focus for the last eight years. Rapha's clubhouses are probably the ultimate manifestation of the company's dedication to its community: more than retail spaces, they are hubs for cyclists to get together, organize races, have use of kit and connect with each other.

Does he do this because it's good for business, or a good thing to do? Simon's answer sums up the Kindness Economy philosophy: 'There's no contradiction between social benefit and business benefit, in my book.' The clubhouses are integral, because 'right at the beginning, the idea was that this wasn't going to be a brand that was about product. This was going to be a brand that was about experience.'

Here is a story that absolutely encapsulates the lovely cause-and-effect of community in action.

In Sydney a couple of years ago a man came up to Simon and said, 'I love the RCC, it's changed my cycling life.'

'That's great. Why is that?' asked Simon.

'Well, it's not just the products, because the products are great, but I've got loads of products. I've got thousands of cycling jerseys. So it's not that. And it's not that I can hang out and have coffee in the clubhouse so much,' he said. 'The thing that you give me that no other brand gives me is memories and friendships.'

What a fantastic evocation of the power and value of community. It's a vindication of Simon's entire business model.

As Simon says: 'The memories are all the rides that he does with us, the hanging out and the experience watching racing with us. And then the friendships – people find people . . . they become their best friends. And, actually, when I look at my best friends, my top ten to twenty friends are all riders and we met largely through riding. I think that's what the RCC does.'

That passionate spark inside Simon had led to this moment – a man on the other side of the world brimming with memories and friendships born out of their shared love for the sport. This is a brand that has been hugely successful by any marker – from that initial struggle to raise £140,000, it was sold in 2017 for £200 million.

It has achieved its waymarker ambition of helping to make cycling stylish and cool. But it is perhaps this feeling of community – the 20,000 members sharing the experience – that Simon is most proud of. 'When I set up the Rapha Cycling Club, the whole proposition was about bringing people together, giving them experiences, introducing them to other people and being a real community,' he says.

When it comes to measuring how the business is doing, Simon does all the things you might expect – looks at the numbers, assesses the inputs and outputs, and looks at the NPS (Net Promoter Score). But when it comes to what the brand is putting out into the world, it comes back to relationships.

'That memories and friendships point, that's actually a very highly tuned version of what we want to offer to all our customers,' he tells me. 'We want all of our customers to basically get more out of their cycling life by being related to us. If somebody comes and buys a Rapha jersey and we never hear from them again, that's a disaster. So from a commercial, business, pragmatic, financial reason it's a disaster because your lifetime value is very low. And our lifetime value is really big. And we want to make it bigger and bigger. But also from a customer value point of view, they've not gotten much value out of what we do. You know, ideally, they'd be watching our films and going on our rides and wearing lots of our products, because they're riding more and therefore they're getting this therapy that I enjoy, and memories and friendships.'

For Simon, that's a true measure of success: 'People who ride bikes honestly, people who ride bikes consistently, not like I do, not competitively, but hard. They just ride regularly. It's their habit. They are generally happier, and they are better people. And that's it. Every cyclist I know is generally well adjusted and pretty happy with their lives, which is pretty amazing.'

It's the Kindness Economy in motion – Simon has taken the sense of freedom and wellbeing and goodness he finds in cycling, and radiated it outwards to a worldwide community. Something indeed to be proud of.

*

There you have it. Five stories from five very different businesses. All of them bringing something extra to the game of business.

If they can do it, can you?

TO DO

Spot the Kindness Economy

Now you know what to look for, can you see businesses putting Kindness Economy principles into action?

Spot them in the wild, glean inspiration, hoard and magpie ideas.

The Kindness Economy is a great cross-fertilization of imagination and energy. Who knows who you'll be inspiring in your turn?

11

Measuring Up

So, how do we know how we are doing? It's a deeper question than you might think.

All over the world today there will be women sitting weaving carpets. In simple homes or collectives, in distant mountain villages or built-up suburbs, in countries like Morocco or India, they will be weaving their stories, creativity and artistry into the rugs they are producing. And once they have finished their work, the rugs they've hand-crafted will start their journey across the globe to us.

Often the rugs will be sold by the husband, brother or boss of these women to a carpet dealer and then traded through a chain of markets, to wholesalers who come in search of them. Hand to hand, they will be sold again and again until finally they end up somewhere that you and I can buy them: a shop or website, most probably.

And by the time we come to pay for them, the gap between the price paid to create them (most probably the women were given just a few pounds a day) and what we buy them for – the monetary value placed on artisanal, unique work – will be stark.

The carpet traders who buy the rugs and increase their price with each sale have to travel to find them, will have spent time making connections with people producing them and have a detailed knowledge of knotting, dyeing and weaving techniques. They deserve to be paid for their time. Then there are the people at the end of the chain with websites or shops to maintain, employees and taxes to pay; for every product that flies off their inventory there will be others that stagnate. They've got to make a living.

That's capitalism. It's how the system works. And there's nothing inherently wrong with it – if we leave aside the fact that it's mostly women producing the rugs and women buying them, but men making the profit. Let's put the thorny issue of gender politics and money-making to one side for now.

The challenge we've got to overcome is how to balance enabling all the people in the chain to make a living – without breaking the backs of those lower down the chain or harming the planet. What if children's tiny hands are used to make even finer knots? What happens if toxic dyes are used, or disposed of, irresponsibly? Should we recalibrate where we place economic value in this chain because the women producing the original work are the least paid? And what happens when a company comes in, is able to buy at scale and negotiate consequent price reductions before selling at the usual mark-up: someone in the chain has got to earn less and it's not the company with the buying power, so who is it?

These are the kinds of questions we need to start asking more as we begin to rebuild.

In this book, you've heard a lot about making profit at any cost, and by that I mean money-making without a care for the people or parts of the planet that are impacted by it. Because the first thing we have to accept is that money isn't made in a vacuum. It's made with the help of people. It's created using the earth's resources – from the electricity used to power the plug on the laptop of the web developer to the water washing through huge factories on the other side of the world to produce our clothes. And we can no longer afford to make the kind of profit that is created at any cost regardless of its impact.

But how do we judge our true costs, our true impacts? In business, of course, you will be measuring your profitability. But there is another type of measurement that goes alongside that – what we might call the 'measurement for humanity'.

Measurements for humanity

Let's start at the highest level – with our nations and governments. Up to now governments and nations have assessed progress purely in terms of numbers – units sold, costs incurred and profit created. All wrapped up in GDP. And we know that concerns about the use of GDP as the universal and absolute measure of a country's progress have been raised almost since the moment the concept was created in the early 1930s. Even Simon Kuznets, the economist who invented the concept of GDP, knew it left something out. The questioning voices have continued ever since.

In 1968, Robert Kennedy made a speech on poverty and the limits of GDP as a measure. He said: '. . . the gross national product [GNP] does not allow for the health of our children, the quality of their education or the joy of their play. It does not include the beauty of our poetry or the strength of our marriages, the intelligence of our public debate or the integrity of our public officials. It measures neither our wit nor our courage, neither our wisdom nor our learning, neither our compassion nor our devotion to our country, it measures everything, in short, except that which makes life worthwhile.'

One huge specific thing it leaves out is what is traditionally thought of as 'women's labour'. There is a huge tranche of work that is invisible to GDP data: food on the table, clothes washed and homes cared for. That's just for starters. It also doesn't value raising children or looking after the sick and elderly, the unpaid caring work done in homes and communities worldwide.

GDP cannot see and does not account for any of this labour because people – mostly women – aren't paid for the skills needed to raise responsible, well-adjusted citizens.

Hardly a shock, though, is it? The history of economics is dominated by men, often white men, from prosperous nations in the northern hemisphere. They were so busy theorizing and doing all that hard intellectual work, is it any wonder they didn't notice who was cooking the meals, doing the school run or turning their children into responsible people?

And yet we have clung like limpets to GDP: blindly measuring economic activity to the exclusion of everything else and addicted to an ever-increasing GDP. 'Success' is defined as an upwards economic trajectory. It's also defined as unfettered growth that doesn't value the things we are losing – those metaphorical (and literal) forests we are cutting down.

Businesses, as much as countries, must start to question this more: if we choose to revolve our metrics solely around economic growth, we will become chained to the kind of short-sighted thinking that trades tomorrow's survival for today's gains.

The new metrics

Luckily, lots of clever people have been bending their minds to building useful new metrics that take us beyond financial considerations.

The Eight Forms of Capital is a framework developed by entrepreneurs Ethan Roland and Gregory Landua, to encourage us to think of the financial structure as an ecosystem. They steer us beyond using financial capital as the sole marker, asking us to take into consideration seven further forms of non-monetary capital and how their flow and exchange feeds into the human economy. For them, there are eight forms of capital: financial, material, natural, social, intellectual, experiential, cultural and (interestingly) spiritual. All eight of these weave in and out of each other in a complex pattern, which frees us from an overreliance on monetary value as a measure of worth. How different might the world look if Simon Kuznets had found a way to work these into his GDP framework?

One initiative that tries to do just that, and build a richer framework to national metrics, is the Social Progress Imperative, a US non-profit that produces the Social Progress Index. It strives to bring together into one simple number all the things that are left out of GDP. It measures countries on nine indicators, which are grouped into three categories: basic human needs, foundations of wellbeing, and opportunity.

By folding all nine indicators into one number, it produces a metric as simple as GDP, but far more informative. Measuring and comparing the SPIs of different nations brings some fascinating insights – and if you haven't seen CEO Michael Green's TED talk on the subject, I urge you to look it up.

When I spoke to him, he talked about the value of aggregating all this complex data into one single score: 'You've got to have something that is simple and communicable.' It has to be a meaningful benchmark that can go up and down.

At a national level, this is hugely important: it forces us to look at nations as more than simply machines for growth.

Some governments are bucking the trend of using GDP, and playing what Michael Green refers to as 'a more interesting game'. These include Scotland, New Zealand and Iceland. (And yes – spot the common thread: these are all countries run by women.)

What I find even more fascinating is the work the Social Progress Imperative is doing with businesses. It has partnered with Deloitte's worldwide to work with businesses – from Coca-Cola and Natura cosmetics in the Amazon, to Cargill, to retailers and mining companies. The SPI is there as a geographical measure, so, as Michael told me, 'Any business that has a direct relationship to a community, we can measure the social progress of that community and say, what's the footprint of my business in the communities that matter?'

There are many benefits arising from this, on both sides of the equation. For the business, it helps them manage potential environmental and social risks; it helps them tell their story and to have a good relationship with the community. Fundamentally, it helps them to support the communities they sit within.

The value of the SPI lies in the fact that it is thorough, specific and wide-ranging, but also in its simplicity. It takes into account all the things that financial metrics leave out.

B-Corp and beyond

From a business point of view, one of the most widely accepted measurements of how companies are doing on a social and environmental front is provided by B-Corp, a certification system that assesses businesses for their impact, believing that they can be a force for good. From a consumer point of view, the accreditation provides reassurance that a company is taking its corporate responsibility seriously. From a societal point of view, it looks to business to provide a positive impact in the world.

At Portas, we have recently been going through the process of applying for B-Corp certification. It is an enlightening exercise. It starts with governance: what is your company's mission, ethics, level of transparency to outside scrutiny? It looks inside your company at the structures; what metrics you use. It looks at how you treat your employees – not just how much they are paid or their working conditions, but whether you offer flexibility, what level of financial security employees have, what other benefits and staff initiatives you have. Do you pay attention to your employees' health and wellbeing? Are you diverse and inclusive? One key measure is the disparity between the lowest and the highest paid in the company – a recognition that the vastly overinflated pay of CEOs is a detrimental trend in society.

From there it looks out at your impact in the community – what you are giving back. It looks at your supply chain management, your environmental impact, and your wider initiatives. Everything, in other words, that describes how you as a company choose to show up in the world.

It's been an eye-opening experience: even for a company like ours that has been working towards Kindness Economy principles for the last few years, the deep level of self-scrutiny and self-reflection has been hugely beneficial – a way not just to evaluate how we are doing, but to get a clear picture of where we are putting our energies, and how to get to where we want to be. I recommend it.

But, much as B-Corp is a fantastic tool, we shouldn't be getting our accreditation, breathing a deep sigh of relief and sitting back on our laurels. What B-Corp measures is great, but these are the table stakes. The true Kindness Economy business goes beyond.

For me, it boils down to simple questions that any business owner should ask: Why should the world want you? What are you going to add? It's one thing to minimize our human and planetary impact. But is the ambition simply to reduce? Or is it actually to get to a positive, additive space? Is it possible to identify a single area and ask yourself what is the one thing you're doing in that space that is going to better the world and humanity?

Businesses must create better metrics for themselves that are clear, laser-sharp and tailored to their own organizations. Think of it as your own personal KPI: Kindness Performance Indicator.

Let's take a look at an example. The Dutch jeans brand G-Star is working in one of the most polluting and environmentally unfriendly industries there is. Cotton is a notoriously thirsty and damaging crop, and the denim industry in particular uses processes, dyes and chemicals that leave an eye-watering impact on the environment.

But since 2006, G-Star have been trying to create the most sustainable denim possible. They use 100 per cent organic cotton, requiring 91 per cent less water and 62 per cent less energy to grow than the average cotton-making process. They have revolutionized the indigo dyeing process, dramatically reducing the amount of chemicals, energy and water needed, and cutting out salts entirely. They commit to ensuring that 98 per cent of their water is recycled, and 2 per cent evaporates, meaning they are not dumping harmful waste water into the environment. They have thought of everything, right down to the buttons (which they make without electroplating in order to eliminate toxic sludge).

The real wow factor, however, lies not in the processes themselves, but in the fact that G-Star have open-sourced their whole approach, hoping to change the entire denim industry. By changing their own practices, they have upskilled their suppliers, and made sure their processes are available to anybody else in the denim industry who wants to use them. They have taken these ideas – ideas in which they've invested hugely over more than a decade – and instead of using them for a competitive edge, they have raised the bar across the board.

They are making jeans – great jeans, as it happens. And, at the same time, they are leaving the world a little better than they found it. Now we need to learn how to measure this kind of impact and create metrics that show how businesses are making a real difference.

Keep asking questions

Tempting as it is to put in place a mission statement, construct a manifesto, make sure the metrics match up to it, roll out the necessary changes and be satisfied, part of the measuring-up process involves constantly scrutinizing your behaviour and re-asking the question: 'Is it enough?'

BrewDog, as we know, is a company that puts its money where its (very vocal) mouth is when it comes to being a revolutionary business, and one of its clear tenets has always been its commitment to the planet. This was an absolutely central plank of its founding philosophy. As co-founder James Watt likes to say, 'It's OK if the business fails; it's not OK if the planet fails.'

From its inception, James and his partner Martin focused on taking plastic out of the supply chain, built local breweries where they could to reduce the impact of transportation, channelled used raw materials into other uses (like fertilizer or cattle food), and even launched a protest beer when Donald Trump pulled America out of the Paris Agreement on climate change. As a brand, it felt confident that it was one of the good guys.

But then everything changed when James and Martin found themselves at a dinner with David Attenborough in early 2020 and began to realize that, far from fixing the world's problems one beer at a time, they were still part of the problem. They needed to go much further, much faster, and make their beer not just carbon neutral but carbon negative. The new aim was to become 'the most sustainable drinks brand on the planet'.

The first thing they did was find an expert, Professor Mike Berners-Lee, who helped them analyse what their actual environmental footprint was, leaving absolutely nothing out. They researched carbon offsetting schemes, before realizing that a lot of them weren't actually all that good. Typically for the brand, they then went the radical route. Deciding that 'our carbon is our problem', they decided to take ownership of the solution, and have bought 2,000 acres of the Scottish Highlands, where they are going to plant 1 million trees to create one of the largest broadleaf forests in Scotland. They have not only embarked on a tree-planting initiative, but will be giving back to the community via sustainable campsites, workshops and retreats. They are using the power built up through community not just to sell beers but actively to push their Make Earth Great Again values.

While this gets underway they are using highly vetted and researched offsetting schemes, and can now claim to remove twice as much CO_2 from the atmosphere as they emit, while still working to drive their emissions down to zero. They are committed to green initiatives throughout their production and distribution chain, using renewable energy to power their plants, an electric delivery fleet, anaerobic digesters to reduce water waste, and a plethora of other initiatives. They did all this while right in the throes of a pandemic. Why? Because they realized that the problem was urgent.

There are two things that particularly strike me: the energy they put into re-examining their model; and their willingness to acknowledge where they fell short. Their sustainability action plan makes this clear: 'We are learning as we go . . . we have made mistakes and we will continue to make mistakes. However, we are willing to rapidly and fundamentally change everything . . .'

Part of the measuring process will involve falling short. But if we are willing to admit where we really are, to pull ourselves up, and to keep trying, then we can create true change.

Changing the framework

Despite huge shifts in perception, in some sectors there is still a tendency to think of metrics for socially progressive initiatives as Scout badges that are nice to have, and will look great on a website, but don't change the fact that the measurement that really matters in the cold hard world of business is your bottom line. (Environmental metrics are somewhat different, not least because in some cases they are chased up by legislation.)

When I spoke to Bevis Watts, the CEO of the ethically driven Triodos Bank, he was convinced that more expansive principles of how we rate the success of organizations can become properly embedded.

For him, it starts with transparency. Clear, accountable – and universal – metrics are vital because they are the only tool a customer has in evaluating what product to go for. And, increasingly, this is what customers demand. 'I do believe that the most successful businesses of the future are the ones that can demonstrate the highest level of social and environmental responsibility to their customers,' he told me.

For their own part, Triodos assess the investments they are presented with via an 'impact prism', an evaluation of the impact of each individual project. The value of this is that it allows them to look at trade-offs within the project (e.g. for food banks or homeless projects 'we might be less focused on their environmental footprint').

Across the bank, they collect relevant data for every project they invest in and aggregate it into their public data. Crucially, their information is as transparent as it can be: once aggregated and carefully audited, it is translated into metrics that 'our deposit customers might better understand – how many homes are powered by the renewable energy generation we finance or how many organic meals are produced annually from the farming and food project we finance'.

All of this hands a measure of control to the customer: the information on the kind of business they are investing with is clearly communicated, something that Bevis believes is key. Without this transparency, how can the customer know what they are buying into? Customers might be less inclined to put their money with banks if they could see that their bank then put them in the same company as oil and tobacco firms, or worse.

Imagine, Bevis Watts says, if banking comparison websites not only listed interest rates, fees and percentages, but gave a clear window into where their money was going and whether that aligned with their stated policies. Making that information freely and routinely available would be transformative. Robust labelling around financial products – just as we have specific labelling on food – would give customers a clear choice about what the money they are depositing is doing.

Michael Green of the SPI agrees: as someone looking for somewhere to bank with, or put his pension, 'I don't want to screw our planet or our society or my kids' future, but what I lack is a way of knowing where to put my money.'

The world is moving towards more universal transparent measurements. Triodos, for instance, helped the United Nations develop their Principles for Responsible Banking – a suite of rules that are designed to assist the banking industry in demonstrating its commitment to sustainable issues, and provide a framework for better behaviour. The principles are useful and instructive – including, importantly, their emphasis on target setting, transparency and accountability.

But while there is now much more accountability when it comes to carbon emissions, energy labelling and environmental footprints, we are badly in need of a common methodology of measurement. As Bevis Watts told me: too many people are making net zero carbon pledges without fully understanding what that entails.

There is also a lot less measurement in the area where, I would argue, we need it even more – the impact our business activities have on humanity itself. Michael Green puts it pithily: 'Any fool can come up with a benchmark, but the question is, does the benchmark tell you something that's really meaningful? . . . In the environment piece we're getting a better handle at least on the carbon issue. But so many ways of measuring the performance of businesses are so spongy on the social side. Often, we're measuring the inputs, or measuring companies on their corporate philanthropy rather than the real contribution of the business.' The process has to be rigorous. 'Otherwise it's a superficial benchmark.' Hear, hear.

A business will map out a vision, ensure it aligns with a core philosophy, and put it into action. But unless we hold ourselves up to our own honest scrutiny, we risk it all being for nothing. Are we measuring up? Only if we make sure that, just as Robert Kennedy so beautifully expressed, we really are measuring the things that make our lives, and our businesses, worthwhile.

We need a useful, practical, universal way of measuring what we are doing to ourselves and to our planet. We need a measurement for humanity.

TO DO
Keep track

At the end of the last chapter, I asked you to look out into the world and identify the people and businesses who are painting the Kindness Economy into existence. We learn by the power of example, but simply observing is not going to be enough. The Kindness Economy's most important goal is to create a movement that harnesses all these learnings and shares them for the greater good. If we want to truly embed these principles into our own lives and businesses, we have to find a way to measure our progress. But how?

There isn't a one-size-fits-all answer to this question: there are as many different outcomes and different types of measurements as there are different organizations. But through all the inspirational people and businesses I have met on this journey, and for all their differences, I have noticed some commonalities about the questions they ask to hold themselves to account, which in turn creates a culture of 'we all drive positive change'. So, let's start there.

Set your goals

Look at the key principles of the Kindness Economy: interconnectedness; values; community; creativity.

- In each principle, ask yourself what goals can you set, either personally or professionally.

- Can you make them very specific, as G-Star did with denim? Make sure the goals are specific to you, or to your business.

- Can you bring things right down to details, as Sheep Inc. did with their supply chain?

- Have you established who makes up your community? How, specifically, can you serve them? What role do they play in reaching your goal?

- Have you looked at all your relationships? Would you like to make them more respectful? Inclusive? Equal?

- How can you build creativity into your business? Into your life? Into your community?

- Prioritize the goals that will have the most impact.

Scrutinize your processes

In each principle, look carefully at the structure and processes of your organization. What processes do you have in place to ensure that your goals in all these areas will be met?

- Who do you include in your decision-making? Why and how?

- Which people are taking responsibility?

- And how are you embracing personal accountability?

- Do you need to create a new role or adapt an old one to drive these goals through your organization? Just as businesses now have Heads of Diversity, a role that didn't exist a decade ago, can you look forward to see what roles your businesses will need in the future? (Timpson has a Director of Happiness, for instance.)

● How, and what type and how often, do you share information?

● Is the direction of information and communication regularly coming from the top of your organization?

Share your ambitions

One surefire way to move aims up your priority list is to make them public. With that in mind, once you have set your goals, ask yourself these questions:

● Are you sharing your commitments and beliefs inside and outside the organization?

● Are your people aware of the company's purpose, goals and expectations?

● Set a timescale, and make it public. I love the expression 'dreams with a deadline'.

● Has it truly landed? Check in with people; are they clear but also excited and motivated?

Check in regularly

- Talk to the people who are most responsible for your goals. At Portas, we do this weekly.

- Make sure the chains of communication are open and working in both directions.

- Ensure that your goals are always up-to-date. This is a shifting landscape.

- Be consistent and keep this a priority.

These measurements are more than a benchmark of how to become a successful and progressive business. By putting these into your daily actions you start to create a deeper relationship with nature, the planet and humanity.

Afterword: My Rallying Cry

My journey towards the Kindness Economy has been years in the making. It started very much privately, as I began to question why I was living the way I was. Then my thoughts moved outwards towards how I work, my business, and the culture I'd created – softer around the edges, particularly in recent years, but at its core still based on alpha values like competition, individual progress, and ever increasing financial growth.

So I did some soul-searching. I read, talked, questioned, and realized that by integrating women's values, strengths and needs, business could be bettered – for women, yes, but absolutely for men too. It was time to recentre the so-called 'soft skills' like collaboration, resilience and empathy which had been undervalued for so long.

I wrapped up all that thinking into *Work Like a Woman* and sat back thinking my work was done.

That smug face lasted all of five minutes.

Because no matter how progressive our internal working cultures might be, nothing can truly change if the larger system we are operating within, and the values it perpetuates, don't also change. And, alongside politics and economics, business is a vital part of that system – one I've been committed to for many decades. Everything it embodies has a concrete impact on people and the natural world.

And so, with my team, I started to pull together the thinking behind the Kindness Economy. We realized it was a natural evolution: we'd rebuilt the internal culture of our own business, helped other businesses to do the same – and now we needed to examine how our newfound values could radiate outwards. We started thinking about how other companies too could transform their behaviours to better impact the world and humanity – and, critically, not get left behind by a consumer culture slowly but surely expecting, wanting, buying into better.

So there we were: me and the Portas team shouting from the rooftops. Our message: it's not only possible to build healthy businesses that do less bad and add more good, it's a commercial imperative. At first, not many people listened. Or mistook it for a 'millennial marketing' effort. Then businesses started coming to us for ideas. The family-owned companies had this ethos baked into their organizations. They think generationally as well as seasonally. I vividly remember working with the wonderful John Smedley, still a family-owned company, and the CEO telling me: 'I am just a custodian of the business.' I love that.

There were shards of inspiration to be found everywhere, once we started looking. From banks to beer makers; small, nimble start-ups to big businesses trying their best to reorientate – there were and *are* businesses out there doing things in new, progressive ways. The Covid conscience has, of course, acted as a catalyst.

But it's nowhere near enough yet. And that is why we all need to pull behind this new value system; from a movement of individual one-offs, to something much larger and more cohesive. Shape the system itself. The way we do things in our business lives and in our personal lives. The baseline from which we all operate.

It's only from this kind of sea change into the 'why' of

what we're doing that business will become a force for so much more good than it is now. And by interlinking with other sectors – from politics to charities and community organizations – we can work towards a common goal of betterment.

That is an amazingly ambitious goal, I know. Will I see its fruition in my lifetime? Probably not. True systemic change takes decades to achieve. The one thing I know, however, that can change rapidly is us. People. We've proved that during the pandemic. And we are at the heart of all these systems, processes, politics and companies. The real change will start inside each one of us.

As I write this, it feels as if I've come full circle because a quote I used at the end of *Work Like a Woman* is as relevant here as it ever was. It's by the great Alice Walker who said: 'The most common way people give up their power is by thinking they don't have any.'

And this is the most important thing to leave you with: that each of us has the power to create change. History has shown us that. Shifts happen when enough individual people knit together to create a larger force. But we lost touch with a sense of our own power in a world that had become so large, frenetic and out of our reach in so many ways. Covid, for all the profound loss it has sparked, enabled us to start embracing our power again: we know how much potential impact each of us can have on the greater whole when we all fly in the same direction.

Covid also gave us the chance to disconnect from the usual rhythms and take a breath. And in that collective moment of slowing down, many of us realized what's really important in life: the health and wellbeing of ourselves and the people we love, and the rhythms of nature on this beautiful planet.

166

It's this new perspective we must cling on to as we start to rebuild, protect it as fiercely as we would a newborn creature to ensure it doesn't slip slowly from our grasp in the coming months and years. The twin parts of acknowledging our power and realizing what is truly important have the potential to be the ultimate salve to the pandemic. Instead of a legacy of grief, disadvantage and fear, Covid has the potential to leave something far more positive behind if we better embrace our individual, joined-up power.

But first we must consciously unknit so much of what we've been taught to value and strive for during recent decades. I'll say it once more here because it's key for us all to realize that every pound we spend – and make – really is a vote for how we want to live. We can make ourselves heard when we deliberately and consciously buy into – as well as start, run or work in – businesses that reflect our values.

Running in parallel to this external shift in our behaviours must be an internal process too – starting with accepting our full selves with compassion, courage and curiosity, letting go of the unrealistic goals we've set and unhelpful ideas we've clung on to. We must tilt our gaze towards progress and fruitfulness, not growth and productivity: 'The rhythm of inspired action, collaboration and rest,' as transformation expert Tara-Nicholle Nelson says.

It's often said that the planet is the greatest gift we've been given. It is, of course. But so is our humanity: our ability to reflect, adapt and empathize. Put these two at the heart of everything you do and you will start to question how you consume and buy, how you do business.

So I call out to everyone to use this power. To question: 'Who do I work for?', 'How do I buy?', 'How do I want to live?' and 'What world do I want to leave my children?' Answer these questions well, and we have the potential to be the glue that could knit all these disparate parts into a true movement for change.

We must guard against our beliefs becoming weaponized in the way that they so often are right now. This is not the Righteous Economy. There is no need to waste energy criticizing the choices of others, attempting to make your argument the loudest or judging others for falling short. It's an essential truth that united we stand, divided we fall. We cannot allow the bigger picture to be hijacked by mobilizing one person against another in the pursuit of moral supremacy.

Politicians, spiritualists, philosophers and everyone in between have been questioning our current system, and the dubious use of economic tools to measure how we're doing, for decades. I am just one of many voices. You can be one too. That's the most important thing I want to leave you with. Because together our individual voices will become a chorus that cannot go unheard.

Notes

p.4   **In 2010, a Mulberry Alexa bag would cost you £695:**
http://fashion.telegraph.co.uk/news-features/TMG7760115/
Mulberry-does-it-again.html

p.4   **Now it's £1,095**: https://www.mulberry.com/gb/shop/
sustainable-icons/alexa-black-heavy-grain

p.5   **Each year £140 million worth of clothing goes into
landfill:** https://wrap.org.uk/resources/guide/textiles/clothing

p.6   **'Our reckless actions have burned the house we live in
. . . we incited Prometheus and buried Pan':** https://www.
gucci.com/uk/en_gb/st/stories/inspirations-and-codes/article/
notes-from-the-silence

p.6   **'Awareness is rapidly changing and I believe we are on
the edge of a fundamental reshaping of finance':** https://
www.blackrock.com/uk/individual/larry-fink-ceo-letter

p.7   **One person who has really helped me to open my eyes
further to the drawbacks of our current economic model is
the economist Kate Raworth:** *The Kindness Economy* podcast: Kate
Raworth and Doughnut Economics https://podcasts.apple.com/
gb/podcast/kate-raworth-and-doughnut-economics/id146303455
3?i=1000510579171

p.9   **'We've been trading off the planet against profit, living
for today and leaving it to others to pay tomorrow':** The Reith
lectures 2020 https://downloads.bbc.co.uk/radio4/reith2020/
Reith_2020_Lecture_4_transcript.pdf

p.10 **22 per cent of the world's population live in poverty – 9.2 per cent in extreme poverty**: https://www.worldvision.org/sponsorship-news-stories/global-poverty-facts

p.10 **the top 1 per cent own almost half (43 per cent) of global wealth:** https://climateandcapitalism.com/2020/12/06/richest-1-own-43-of-global-wealth/

p.10 **Roughly 3.2 billion people worldwide are impacted by land degradation:** https://en.unesco.org/news/worsening-land-degradation-impacts-32-billion-people-worldwide

p.10 **At roughly 416 parts per million, carbon dioxide levels in our atmosphere:** https://www.co2.earth/

p.10 **over 5 million people in the UK were paid less than a fair living wage:** https://www.livingwage.org.uk/news/news-more-5-million-uk-workers-paid-below-real-living-wage

p.10 **Half of the world's forests have been cleared:** https://www.theworldcounts.com/challenges/planet-earth/forests-and-deserts/rate-of-deforestation/story

p.10 **12–17 per cent of annual global greenhouse gas emissions:** https://www.theworldcounts.com/stories/consequences_of_depletion_of_natural_resources

p.10 **1 million marine animals are killed by plastic every year, while less than 9 per cent of all the plastic produced is recycled:** https://plasticoceans.ca/wp-content/uploads/2021/02/Plastic-Oceans-Canada-2020-Report.pdf

p.11 **20 per cent of the world's population are responsible for the consumption of 80 per cent of its resources:** https://www.activesustainability.com/environment/natural-resources-deficit/

p.11 **We've got greater inequality**: https://www.un.org/en/un75/inequality-bridging-divide

p.11 **In the US, the number of teens reporting the symptoms of depression increased by 52 per cent:** https://www.npr.org/sections/health-shots/2019/03/14/703170892/a-rise-in-depression-among-teens-and-young-adults-could-be-linked-to-social-medi?t=1617979360115

p.13 **The Nobel Prize-winning economist Robert Shiller:** Shiller, Robert, *Narrative Economics: How Stories Go Viral and Drive Major Economic Events* (Princeton University Press, 2019)

p.14 **'When we use the earth's resources . . . ':** https://www.ted.com/talks/the_ted_interview_kate_raworth_argues_that_rethinking_economics_can_save_our_planet

p.14 **'Economic growth accompanied by worsening social outcomes is not success. It is failure':** https://www.globalcitizen.org/en/content/jacinda-ardern-goalkeepers-unga-2019/

p.15 **the task is to be hospice workers for the dying culture and midwives for the new:** https://oac.cdlib.org/findaid/ark:/13030/kt3c601926/

p.16 **In 2013, when the late writer David Foster Wallace gave a commencement speech:** https://fs.blog/2012/04/david-foster-wallace-this-is-water/

p.16 **'The way we see things is affected by what we know or what we believe':** Berger, John, *Ways of Seeing* (Penguin, 1972)

p.19 **'Covid-19 will destroy many things, but hopefully too the broken scaffolding of our moral imagination':** https://www.theguardian.com/commentisfree/2021/mar/17/rich-countries-hoarding-vaccines-us-eu-africa

p.21 **'elastic thinking':** Mlodinow, Leonard, *Elastic* (Penguin, 2019)

p.22 **Asda invested £2 million into an initiative to provide 7,000 Dell laptops to schoolchildren:** https://corporate.asda.

com/20210121/were-providing-7-000-dell-laptops-to-help-schools-tackle-digital-exclusion

p.22 **The Co-op instituted an 'I've got time to chat' badge:** https://centralengland.coop/press-and-media/ive-got-time-to-chat-scheme-rolled-out-by-central-england-co-op-as-part-of-effort-to-tackle-isolation-and-loneliness

p.22 **'Nothing is fixed . . . The sea rises . . .':** Baldwin, James, *Nothing Personal* (Beacon Press, 1964)

p.23 **catastrophic write-downs of 2020 and 2021:** https://www.theguardian.com/business/2021/mar/11/john-lewis-may-not-reopen-some-stores-as-chain-slumps-to-517m-loss

p.23 **More than 17,500 chain stores shut in 2020:** https://www.theguardian.com/business/2021/mar/14/great-britain-high-streets-lost-more-than-17500-chain-stores-in-2020-covid

p.25 **The co-founder of Lush cosmetics, Mark Constantine, called it 'the Covid rinse':** *The Kindness Economy* podcast: Making the Beauty Industry More Than Skin Deep with Mark Constantine https://podcasts.apple.com/gb/podcast/making-beauty-industry-more-than-skin-deep-mark-constantine/id1463034553?i=1000506841615

p.27 **Philosopher Gershom Scholem called them 'the plastic hours':** https://www.amacad.org/news/americas-plastic-hour

p.27 **Carlo Rovelli observes in *The Order of Time*:** Rovelli, Carlo, *The Order of Time* (Penguin, 2019)

p.27 **'Discomfort is a proxy for progress':** Novogratz, Jacqueline, *Manifesto for a Moral Revolution* (St Martin's Press, 2020)

p.29 ***Thinking in Systems* by Donella H. Meadows:** Meadows, Donella H., *Thinking in Systems: A Primer* (Chelsea Green Publishing, 2008)

p.29 ***On Being*** with **Krista Tippett:** https://podcasts. apple.com/us/podcast/on-being-with-krista-tippett/id1508 92556

p.30 ***Reality Is Not What It Seems*** by **Carlo Rovelli:** Rovelli, Carlo, *Reality Is Not What It Seems: The Journey to Quantum Gravity* (Allen Lane, 2016)

p.30 ***Can't Get You Out of My Head***: https://www.imdb.com/ title/tt13973190/

p.30 ***My Octopus Teacher***: https://www.netflix.com/gb/title/ 81045007

p.30 ***GABA*** **podcast:** https://podcasts.apple.com/gb/podcast/ gaba/id1480815448

p.30 ***Gratitude*** by **Oliver Sacks:** Sacks, Oliver, *Gratitude* (Picador, 2015)

p.30 ***The Untethered Soul: The Journey Beyond Yourself*** by **Michael Singer:** Singer, Michael, *The Untethered Soul: The Journey Beyond Yourself* (New Harbinger Publications, 2007)

p.30 ***A Thousand Mornings*** by **Mary Oliver:** Oliver, Mary, *A Thousand Mornings* (Corsair, 2018)

p.30 ***A Bus Pass Named Desire*** by **Christopher Matthew:** Matthew, Christopher, *A Bus Pass Named Desire* (Little, Brown, 2016)

p.30 ***Kids Write Jokes***: https://twitter.com/KidsWriteJokes

p.31 **@loveofhuns:** https://www.instagram.com/loveofhuns/

p.31 ***Ten Percent Happier*** with **Dan Harris:** https://www. tenpercent.com/podcast

p.31 **'You Can't Have It All' by Barbara Ras:** https://poets. org/poem/you-cant-have-it-all From Ras, Barbara, *Bite Every Sorrow: Poems* (LSU Press, 1998)

p.31 ***What Matters Most: Living a More Considered Life* by James Hollis:** Hollis, James, *What Matters Most: Living a More Considered Life* (Gotham Books, 2008)

p.31 ***The Diving-Bell and the Butterfly* by Jean-Dominique Bauby:** Bauby, Jean-Dominique, *The Diving-Bell and the Butterfly* (Fourth Estate, 1997)

p.31 **'Small Kindnesses' by Danusha Laméris:** http://www. danushalameris.com/poems.html First published in *Healing the Divide: Poems of Kindness and Connection*, James Crews (ed.) (Green Place Books, 2020)

p.31 ***Little Dieter Needs to Fly*:** https://www.imdb.com/title/ tt0145046/

p.33 **So when I was commissioned by the government to look into the state of the high street:** The Portas Review, December 2011 https://assets.publishing.service.gov.uk/ government/uploads/system/uploads/attachment_data/ file/6292/2081646.pdf

p.36 **Chartwells, the catering company involved:** https:// www.bbc.co.uk/news/business-55931994

p.36 **Uber drivers using the legal system to change the entire employment model of the company:** https://www.bbc.co.uk/ news/business-56123668

p.36 **US shoppers boycotting the brands and stores that didn't meaningfully support the BLM movement:** https:// www.bbc.com/worklife/article/20200612-black-lives-matter-do- companies-really-support-the-cause

p.37 **James Watt is a hugely successful businessman:** *The Kindness Economy* podcast: Creating a New Type of Business with James Watt https://podcasts.apple.com/gb/podcast/creating-a-new-kind-of-business-with-james-watt/id1463034553?i=1000506015204

p.37 **BrewDog was built on the principle of listening to its customers:** https://www.brewdog.com/uk/community/culture/our-history

p.38 **There are currently 180,000 members of this community:** https://www.brewdog.com/blog/efp-tomorrow-extended

p.44 **940 per cent increase in CEO compensation over the past forty years:** https://corporate-rebels.com/stop-this-madness-it-s-time-to-end-ridiculous-ceo-pay/

p.44 **Top bosses now earn 117 times the annual pay of the average worker:** https://www.bbc.co.uk/news/business-49411245

p.45 **Right now, 77 per cent of people globally say they value decency in business as much as price and convenience:** https://fashionunited.com/news/retail/effects-of-covid-19-consumers-value-trust-reputation-and-conversation/2020042233225

p.45 **I stood on stage in London to give a TED talk:** https://www.ted.com/talks/mary_portas_welcome_to_the_kindness_economy

p.47 **The economist Manfred Max-Neef tells us:** https://www.zinnedproject.org/materials/rethinking-the-economy

p.47 **drawn by the psychologist Andrew Solomon in his book on parenting diverse children:** Solomon, Andrew, *Far from the Tree: Parents, Children and the Search for Identity* (Scribner, 2013)

p.53 **The majority (51 per cent) of Gen Z research a brand's corporate social responsibility (CSR) practices before buying:** https://www.marketingdive.com/news/post-truth-climate-impacts-gen-zs-conflicting-brand-perceptions-forrest/593640/

p.53 **58 per cent of people say they want brands to be a positive force in shaping culture:** https://www.edelman.com/news-awards/brand-trust-2020-press-release

p.53 **61 per cent would like them to work towards making the future better than the present:** https://www.edelman.com/news-awards/brand-trust-2020-press-release

p.53 **57 per cent are more likely to buy from brands that support their community:** https://www.ey.com/en_uk/news/2020/04/new-consumer-categories-emerge-as-covid-19-fundamentally-changes-the-way-people-shop-and-buy

p.53 **55 per cent – more than half of UK shoppers – now consider the impact of clothing production on the environment to be 'severe':** https://archive.wrap.org.uk/sites/files/wrap/Clothing-Behaviours-During-Covid-19-Report-wave2.pdf

p.55 **'Civilization is revving itself into a pathologically short attention span . . . ':** https://longnow.org/about/

p.55 **The philosopher Roman Krznaric points to a need for 'cathedral thinking':** Krznaric, Roman, *The Good Ancestor* (Ebury, 2020)

p.55 **As Daniel Kahneman pointed out in *Thinking, Fast and Slow*:** Kahneman, Daniel, *Thinking, Fast and Slow* (Penguin, 2012)

p.56 **For a historical example, look to the great Quaker businesses of the nineteenth century:** http://dooy.info/examples/quaker.capitalism.html

p.58 **The Banksy painting of a little boy:** https://www.bbc.co.uk/news/uk-england-hampshire-56497104

p.59 **80 per cent of people want brands to solve societal problems:** https://www.edelman.com/research/brand-trust-2020

p.59 **84 per cent want brand social channels to facilitate a feeling of community:** https://www.edelman.com/research/covid-19-brand-trust-report

p.59 **'What if each of us gave more to the world than we took from it? Everything would change':** https://www.ted.com/talks/jacqueline_novogratz_what_it_takes_to_make_change/transcript?language=en

p.64 **'Start where you are':** Chodron, Pema, *Start Where You Are* (Element Books, 2005)

p.65 **'Our whole business is based on a culture of trust and kindness':** https://guild.co/blog/better-business-james-timpson-interview/

p.65 **'trusting them to make decisions as they see fit':** https://www.timpson.co.uk/about/careers-at-timpson

p.65 **'I'm as commercial as you get':** https://www.thetimes.co.uk/article/meet-my-secret-weapon-a-director-of-happiness-vqkspsj7x

p.66 **'Just say yes' to customers:** https://www.timpson.co.uk/about/magic-dust

p.67 **'Tweaking your mindset, motivation and habits is about turning your heart toward the fluidity of the world rather than planting your feet on its stability':** David, Susan, *Emotional Agility* (Penguin, 2017) *p.70* '[These are] not actually the soft skills . . . ': *On Being* podcast with Krista Tippett https://onbeing.org/programs/jacqueline-novogratz-towards-a-moral-revolution/

p.74 **According to financial research at Refinitiv Lipper . . . :** https://www.funds-europe.com/news/esg-fund-flows-gain-half-of-market-share

p.74 **doubts about the way Deliveroo treats its workers led to investors getting cold feet:** https://www.investorschronicle.co.uk/news/2021/03/30/fund-managers-express-doubts-ahead-of-deliveroo-s-ipo/

p.75 **Simon Sinek's eminently sensible *Find Your Why*:** Sinek, Simon, *Find Your Why: A Practical Guide for Discovering Purpose for You and Your Team* (Portfolio, 2017)

p.77 **'As a fashion brand we're the first to admit we're behind. In the past we haven't shouted about our efforts . . . ':** https://www.ganni.com/en-gb/responsibility-elephant.html

p.78 **Simon Sinek rightly and famously posited three questions:** Sinek, Simon, *Find Your Why: A Practical Guide for Discovering Purpose for You and Your Team* (Portfolio, 2017)

p.80 **president and CEO of the international healthcare organization Project Hope, Rabih Torbay, echoed Donne's thought as he considered the impact of the pandemic:** https://www.projecthope.org/covid-19-showed-how-interconnected-we-are-to-move-forward-we-must-embrace-it/12/2020/

p.84 **'in an age of radical transparency, your internal culture is your brand':** https://trendwatching.com/quarterly/2017-09/glass-box-brands/

p.85 **it had ignored red flags in its supply chain:** https://www.businessinsider.com/boohoo-ignored-pay-and-working-conditions-red-flags-review-2020-9?r=US&IR=T

p.87   **a remarkable alliance sprang up between giant multinationals McDonald's and Aldi in Germany:** https://www.winsightgrocerybusiness.com/retailers/aldi-mcdonalds-make-staff-sharing-deal-germany

p.87   **the powers that be at MGM announced they would be delaying the release of their juggernaut James Bond film for the second time in October 2020:** https://www.ft.com/content/1545e213-3d92-47e0-ac1b-7d92d39c92b1

p.88   **'We must look at any given situation or problem from the front and from the back . . .':** Dalai Lama, *The Book of Joy* (Hutchinson, 2016)

p.94   **In the UK more than £30 billion worth of clothing sits at the back of wardrobes:** https://archive.wrap.org.uk/content/wrap-reveals-uks-%C2%A330-billion-unused-wardrobe

p.94   **That £140 million worth of clothing in landfill that I referred to earlier? That's 350,000 tonnes a year:** https://wrap.org.uk/resources/report/valuing-our-clothes-true-cost-how-we-design-use-and-dispose-clothing-uk-2012

p.94   **global textile production releasing 1.2 billion tonnes of greenhouse gases into the atmosphere annually:** https://www.ellenmacarthurfoundation.org/assets/downloads/publications/A-New-Textiles-Economy_Full-Report.pdf

p.95   **for every £1 spent on food by British consumers, an extra £1 of hidden costs was incurred . . . :** http://sustainablefoodtrust.org/wp-content/uploads/2013/04/HCOF-Report-online-version.pdf

p.97   **In 2016, they donated all their revenue for the day to environmental causes:** https://eu.patagonia.com/gb/en/stories/record-breaking-black-friday-sales-to-benefit-the-planet/story-31140.html

p.97 'At the end of the year, we measure success by how much good we've done and what impact we're having on society, not by profit': https://www.brandingstrategyinsider.com/brand-patagonia-a-founders-story-and-strategy/

p.97 Black Friday generates massive revenue for the retail sector – £8.6 billion in the UK in 2019: https://www.statista.com/topics/5849/black-friday-in-the-uk/

p.98 PrettyLittleThing's little black dress which went on sale for 8p: https://www.theguardian.com/business/2020/nov/27/critics-slam-pretty-little-things-8p-black-friday-dress-deal

p.98 they partnered with Feeding America to try to provide 2 million meals for people in need: https://www.everlane.com/feeding-america

p.98 Allbirds actually raised their prices on Black Friday: https://www.insider.com/allbirds-black-friday-sale-donating-to-greta-thunberg-climate-change-2020-11

p.98 Swiss bag company Freitag shut its online store entirely on Black Friday: https://media.freitag.ch/en/media/blackfriday

p.99 OVO energy . . . went with a promotion to help people go green on Black Friday: https://www.ovoenergy.com/ovo-newsroom/press-releases/2020/november/black-friday-causes-carbon-chaos-ovo-energy-encourages-brits-to-go-green-this-black-friday.html

p.99 the 61 per cent of shoppers who believe that consumerism around large shopping events has got out of hand: https://uk.finance.yahoo.com/news/brits-could-save-43bn-by-switching-to-secondhand-gifts-this-christmas-070025426.html

p.99 45 per cent of UK consumers said that sustainability was important in their shopping decisions: https://www.

occstrategy.com/en/about-occ/news-and-media/article/
id/5380/2019/12/almost-half-of-uk-consumers-said-a-retailers-
environmental-agenda-was-important-when-shopping

p.103 **'The trust of a city street is formed over time from many, many little public sidewalk contacts . . .':** Jacobs, Jane, *The Death and Life of Great American Cities* (Random House, 1961)

p.103 **Our need for other humans is so strong in fact that the effects of loneliness produce signals in the brain very like those of acute hunger:** https://news.mit.edu/2020/hunger-social-cravings-neuroscience-1123

p.103 **only 53 per cent of Americans report that they have daily meaningful interactions with other people:** https://www.multivu.com/players/English/8294451-cigna-us-loneliness-survey/

p.103 **43 per cent feel isolated from others:** https://www.multivu.com/players/English/8294451-cigna-us-loneliness-survey/

p.103 **Gen Z are the loneliest generation:** https://www.ons.gov.uk/resource?uri=/peoplepopulationandcommunity/wellbeing/articles/lonelinesswhatcharacteristicsandcircumstancesareassociatedwithfeelinglonely/2018-04-10/edca464d.png

p.103 **the government has appointed a Minister for Loneliness:** https://time.com/5248016/tracey-crouch-uk-loneliness-minister/

p.104 **'To thrive, you have to be both an individual . . . You need to be part of something bigger than yourself':** Brandreth, Gyles, *The 7 Secrets of Happiness* (Short Books, 2013)

p.104 **More than a third (36 per cent) of people in Britain predict that they will keep up their increased use of independent local shops when lockdown ends:** https://www.retail-focus.co.uk/over-a-third-of-brits-plan-to-use-their-local-stores-more-after-lockdown/

p.104 **74 per cent of UK businesses plan on maintaining some level of home working into the future:** https://www.bbc.co.uk/news/business-54413214

p.104 **57 per cent of people intend to keep using shops that offer locally produced goods after lockdown has finished:** https://www2.deloitte.com/uk/en/pages/press-releases/articles/three-in-five-consumers-have-used-more-local-stores-and-services-to-support-them-during-lockdown.html

p.104 **In Milan, the mayor is trialling the idea of the 'fifteen-minute city':** https://www.ft.com/content/c1a53744-90d5-4560-9e3f-17ce06aba69a

p.108 **73 per cent of consumers consider customer experience an important factor in their purchasing decisions, and indeed 42 per cent will actually pay more for a friendly, welcoming experience:** https://www.pwc.com/us/en/advisory-services/publications/consumer-intelligence-series/pwc-consumer-intelligence-series-customer-experience.pdf

p.108 **mobile ad blocking rose globally by 64 per cent between 2016 and 2019:** https://www.cnet.com/news/ad-blocking-takes-off-on-mobile-phones-a-challenge-for-publishers/

p.110 **This was live-action interplay between brand and customer:** https://www.wired.co.uk/article/how-to-build-a-brand-glossier

p.111 **Nike feeds back into its roots through its Community Stores:** https://finance.yahoo.com/news/inside-nike-community-store-l-040105674.html

p.114 **'I feel like I've always had an inkling for the future':** *Work Like a Woman* podcast: Sharing the Social Load with

Sharmadean Reid https://www.listennotes.com/podcasts/the-kindness-economy/work-like-a-woman-sharing-CelSFAtovVi/

p.116 '[Kids are] not frightened of being wrong . . . ': https://www.ted.com/talks/sir_ken_robinson_do_schools_kill_creativity/transcript?language=en

p.117 An Australian survey by Xero found that over 50 per cent of businesses that have thrived over the pandemic pointed at gut instinct as the main thing they relied on to get them through: https://www.theguardian.com/xero-resilient-business/2020/sep/09/an-instinct-for-change-how-small-businesses-can-pivot-to-new-possibilities

p.118 'The days of unskilled manual labour exchanged for money will gradually be gone . . .': http://www.publicis.com/news/details/lead-the-change-in-innovation-dylan-williams-global-chief-strategy-innovation-officer-publicis-worldwide/

p.118 education should prioritize the skills of creativity, humanity, wisdom and 'being human': Jack Ma: Teach Kids Creativity https://www.youtube.com/watch?v=5zixvl7j93E

p.119 ex-footballer Lou Macari, who runs a homeless shelter: http://macari-foundation.co.uk/2020/05/11/pods-inside-warehouse-during-coronavirus/

p.121 Sophia Loren's response when she was asked in a *Desert Island Discs* interview what it was like working with Vittorio De Sica: https://www.bbc.co.uk/programmes/m000sgvk

p.122 'human creativity is the ultimate economic resource': Florida, Richard, *The Rise of the Creative Class* (Perseus Book Group, 2002)

p.125–129 All Edzard van der Wyck quotes from interview with author

p.130 **Sheep Inc. won a Drapers Sustainable Fashion Award:** https://sustainablefashion.drapersonline.com/winners-2021

p.130 **a commitment to make sure everyone who supplies goods or services to the company earns at least a fair living wage . . . by 2030:** https://www.unilever.com/news/press-releases/2021/unilever-commits-to-help-build-a-more-inclusive-society.html

p.130 **They are aiming for net zero carbon from their own operations by 2030:** https://www.unilever.com/news/news-and-features/Feature-article/2021/why-we-are-putting-our-climate-plans-to-a-shareholder-vote.html

p.131 **'Everything we do through our business and our brands must be underpinned by an absolute commitment to respect human rights':** https://www.unilever.com/Images/unilever-human-rights-report-2020_tcm244-558516_en.pdf

p.131 **Unilever's Sustainable Living Plan was put in place by Alan Jope's predecessor, Paul Polman:** https://www.reutersevents.com/sustainability/farewell-paul-polman-epitome-twenty-first-century-ceo

p.131 **values firmly rooted in social responsibility 'is *definitely* going to become a reason for people to preferentially choose our brands':** https://www.bbc.co.uk/programmes/m000rc41

p.131 **'Without healthy societies, we don't have a healthy business':** https://www.bbc.co.uk/news/business-55735108

p.132 **'Our first priority is our employees . . . Then we take care of our customers and consumers, our business partners, the planet, the societies we do business in . . . ':** https://www.pioneerspost.com/news-views/20210122/unilever-takes-on-·····lity-trailblazing-supply-chain-targets

p.132 'To break down stereotypes and make everybody feel included . . . ': Aline Santos correspondence with author, March 2021

p.132 the Unstereotype Alliance, launched in conjunction with UN Women and other industry leaders in 2017: https://www.unilever.com/news/press-releases/2017/launch-of-unstereotype-alliance-set-to-eradicate-outdated-stereotypes-in-advertising.html

p.133 'I like making profit': *The Kindness Economy* podcast: Making the Beauty Industry More Than Skin Deep with Mark Constantine https://podcasts.apple.com/gb/podcast/making-beauty-industry-more-than-skin-deep-mark-constantine/id1463034553?i=1000506841615

p.134 'I just think most people when they work here . . .': Mark Constantine interview with author, March 2021

p.134 'Recreating a dynamic environment, greening the desert': *The Kindness Economy* podcast: Making the Beauty Industry More Than Skin Deep with Mark Constantine https://podcasts.apple.com/gb/podcast/making-beauty-industry-more-than-skin-deep-mark-constantine/id1463034553?i=1000506841615

p.135 'Both: what I do is gather lots of opinions. I don't have a lot of opinions of my own.': Mark Constantine interview with author, March 2021

p.135 'The vision and the culture of my business is provided by the people within it.': *The Kindness Economy* podcast: Making the Beauty Industry More Than Skin Deep with Mark Constantine https://podcasts.apple.com/gb/podcast/making-beauty-industry-more-than-skin-deep-mark-constantine/id1463034553?i=1000506841615

p.136 'I worked with another colleague on the maternity benefit . . .': Mark Constantine interview with author, March 2021

p.136–139 All Peter Oliver quotes from interview with author, March 2021

p.140–144 All Simon Mottram quotes from interview with author, March 2021

p.148 '. . . the gross national product [GNP] does not allow for the health of our children . . .': https://www.jfklibrary.org/learn/about-jfk/the-kennedy-family/robert-f-kennedy/robert-f-kennedy-speeches/remarks-at-the-university-of-kansas-march-18-1968

p.150 The Eight Forms of Capital is a framework developed by entrepreneurs Ethan Roland and Gregory Landua: http://thegoodliferevival.com/blog/eight-forms-of-capital

p.150 the Social Progress Imperative, a US non-profit that produces the Social Progress Index: https://www.socialprogress.org/

p.150 CEO Michael Green's TED talk on the subject: https://www.ted.com/talks/michael_green_what_the_social_progress_index_can_reveal_about_your_country?language=en

p.150 'You've got to have something that is simple and communicable': *The Kindness Economy* podcast: Measuring Progress with Michael Green https://podcasts.apple.com/gb/podcast/measuring-progress-with-michael-green-a-portas-round-table/id1463034553?i=1000512505486

p.151 It has partnered with Deloitte's worldwide to work with businesses: https://www2.deloitte.com/global/en/pages/about-deloitte/articles/social-progress-imperative-index.html

p.151 B-Corp, a certification system that assesses businesses for their impact: https://bcorporation.uk/

p.153 **since 2006, G-Star have been trying to create the most sustainable denim possible:** https://www.g-star.com/en_gb/about-us/responsibility/sustainable-product

p.154 **BrewDog, as we know, is a company that puts its money where its (very vocal) mouth is:** *The Kindness Economy* podcast: Creating a New Type of Business with James Watt https://podcasts.apple.com/gb/podcast/creating-a-new-kind-of-business-with-james-watt/id1463034553?i=1000506015204

p.154 **focused on taking plastic out of the supply chain, built local breweries where they could to reduce the impact of transportation, channelled used raw materials into other uses . . .:** https://www.brewdog.com/blog/brewdog-tomorrow-a-sustainability-update

p.155 **actively to push their Make Earth Great Again values:** https://d1fnkk8n0t8a0e.cloudfront.net/docs/Make-Earth-Great-Again_4.pdf

p.157 **'I do believe that the most successful businesses of the future are the ones that can demonstrate the highest level of social and environmental responsibility to their customers':** *The Kindness Economy* podcast: Your Money Can Save the World with Bevis Watts https://podcasts.apple.com/gb/podcast/your-money-can-change-the-world-with-bevis-watts/id1463034553?i=1000509634441

p.157 **'we might be less focused on their environmental footprint'** and **'our deposit customers might better understand . . .':** Bevis Watts correspondence with author, March 2021

p.158 **'I don't want to screw the planet or our society or my kids' future':** *The Kindness Economy* podcast: Measuring Progress with Michael Green https://podcasts.apple.com/gb/podcast/measuring-progress-with-michael-green-a-portas-round-table/id1463034553?i=1000512505486

p.162 **Timpson has a Director of Happiness, for instance:** https://www.thetimes.co.uk/article/meet-my-secret-weapon-a-director-of-happiness-vqkspsj7x

p.167 **'The rhythm of inspired action, collaboration and rest':** https://www.taranicholle.com/

Acknowledgements

With heartfelt thanks to the women who make me look good, time and again – Caireen and Lilli, my leading women and partners in crime at Portas, who helped make the Kindness Economy and this book a reality. I'm never short of ideas when I know you two can make them happen. To Andrea, my editor, for spotting and always supporting my ideas, and Celia, for your poise, patience – and for bringing such method to the madness.